C0-APF-494

Cram101 Textbook Outlines to accompany:

Theoretical Criminology

Vold and Bernard and Snipes, 5th Edition

An Academic Internet Publishers (AIPI) publication (c) 2007.

Cram101 and Cram101.com are AIPI publications and services. All notes, highlights, reviews, and practice tests are prepared by AIPI for use in AIPI publications, all rights reserved.

You have a discounted membership at www.Cram101.com with this book.

Get all of the practice tests for the chapters of this textbook, and access in-depth reference material for writing essays and papers. Here is an example from a Cram101 Biology text:

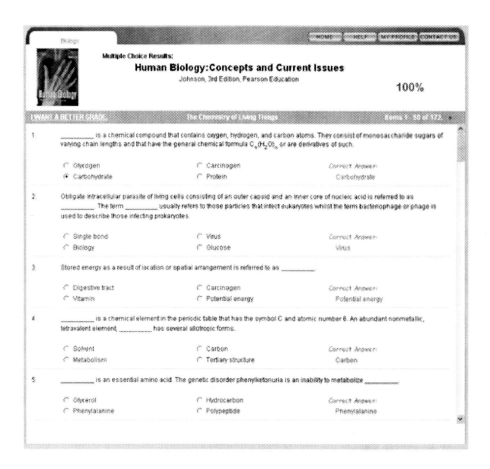

When you need problem solving help with math, stats, and other disciplines, www.Cram101.com will walk through the formulas and solutions step by step.

With Cram101.com online, you also have access to extensive reference material.

You will nail those essays and papers. Here is an example from a Cram101 Biology text:

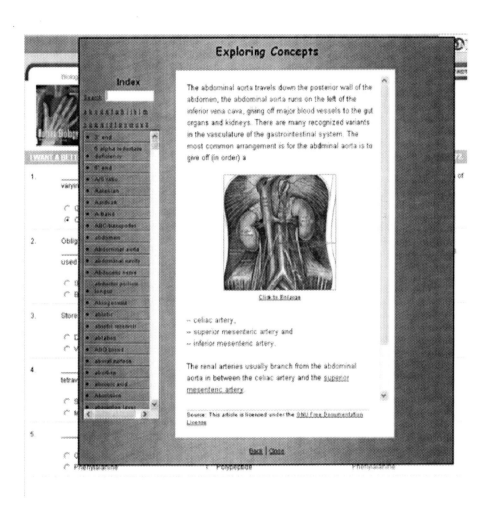

Visit **www.Cram101.com**, click Sign Up at the top of the screen, and enter DK73DW2378 in the promo code box on the registration screen. Access to www.Cram101.com is normally $9.95, but because you have purchased this book, your access fee is only $4.95. Sign up and stop highlighting textbooks forever.

Learning System

Cram101 Textbook Outlines is a learning system. The notes in this book are the highlights of your textbook, you will never have to highlight a book again.

How to use this book. Take this book to class, it is your notebook for the lecture. The notes and highlights on the left hand side of the pages follow the outline and order of the textbook. All you have to do is follow along while your intructor presents the lecture. Circle the items emphasized in class and add other important information on the right side. With Cram101 Textbook Outlines you'll spend less time writing and more time listening. Learning becomes more efficient.

Cram101.com Online

Increase your studying efficiency by using Cram101.com's practice tests and online reference material. It is the perfect complement to Cram101 Textbook Outlines. Use self-teaching matching tests or simulate in-class testing with comprehensive multiple choice tests, or simply use Cram's true and false tests for quick review. Cram101.com even allows you to enter your in-class notes for an integrated studying format combining the textbook notes with your class notes.

Visit **www.Cram101.com**, click Sign Up at the top of the screen, and enter **DK73DW2378** in the promo code box on the registration screen. Access to www.Cram101.com is normally $9.95, but because you have purchased this book, your access fee is only $4.95. Sign up and stop highlighting textbooks forever.

Copyright © 2007 by Academic Internet Publishers, Inc. All rights reserved. "Cram101"® and "Never Highlight a Book Again!"® are registered trademarks of Academic Internet Publishers, Inc. The Cram101 Textbook Outline series is printed in the United States. ISBN: 1-4288-1711-5

Theoretical Criminology
Vold and Bernard and Snipes, 5th

CONTENTS

Crime	Crime refers to any action that violates criminal laws established by political authority. A crime in a nontechnical sense is an act that violates a very important political or moral command.
Sociology of law	Sociology of law is also often conceived of as an approach within legal studies stressing the actual social effects of legal institutions, doctrines, and practices and vice versa. In the latter sense it is also referred to as the "law and society" approach, or even broader as "socio-legal studies".
Punishment	Punishment is the practice of imposing something unpleasant on a subject as a response to some unwanted behavior or disobedience that the subject has displayed.
Criminology	Criminology refers to the systematic study of crime and the criminal justice system, including the police, courts, and prisons.
Attitude	Attitude refers to an enduring mental representation of a person, place, or thing that evokes an emotional response and related behavior.
Criminal justice	Criminal justice refers to the system used by government to maintain social control, enforce laws, and administer justice. Law enforcement (police), courts, and corrections are the primary agencies charged with these responsibilities.
Organization	In sociology organization is understood as planned, coordinated and purposeful action of human beings to construct or compile a common tangible or intangible product or service.
Feudalism	Feudalism refers to a general set of reciprocal legal and military obligations among the warrior nobility of Europe during the Middle Ages, revolving around the three key concepts of lords, vassals, and fiefs.
Social control	A social mechanism that regulates individual and group behavior through sanctions and rewards is a social control.
Social theory	Social theory refers to the use of theoretical frameworks to explain and analyze social patterns and large-scale social structures. Social theory attempts to answer the question 'what is?', not 'what should be?'. One should therefore not confuse it with philosophy or with belief.
Typology	Typology refers to the classification of observations in terms of their attributes on two or more variables. The classification of newspapers as liberal-urban, liberal-rural, conservative-urban, or conservative-rural would be an example of a typology.
Community	Community refers to a group of people who share a common sense of identity and interact with one another on a sustained basis.
Naturalism	An approach to field research based on the assumption that an objective social reality exists and can be observed and reported accurately, is referred to as naturalism.
Sanction	A punishment for nonconformity that reinforces socially approved forms of behavior is a sanction.
Society	A society is a grouping of individuals, which is characterized by common interest and may have distinctive culture and institutions.
Variable	A characteristic that varies in value or magnitude along which an object, individual or group may be categorized, such as income or age, is referred to as a variable.
Scientific revolution	Scientific revolution refers to the replacement of one scientific paradigm with another.
Kuhn	Kuhn is most famous for his book The Structure of Scientific Revolutions (SSR) (1962) in which he presented the idea that science does not progress via a linear accumulation of new knowledge, but instead undergoes periodic revolutions which he calls "paradigm shifts", in which the nature of scientific inquiry within a particular field is abruptly transformed.
Mean	In statistics, mean has two related meanings: a)the average in ordinary English, which is also called the arithmetic mean (and is distinguished from the geometric mean or harmonic mean). The average is

Go to **Cram101.com** for the Practice Tests for this Chapter.
And, **NEVER** highlight a book again!

	also called sample mean. b)the expected value of a random variable, which is also called the population mean.
Negative correlation	A relationship between two variables in which one variable increases as the other decreases, is referred to as a negative correlation.
Classical criminology	Criminology based on both free will and determinism and whose chief aim was to deter crime refers to classical criminology. It was part of the humanist reaction during the Enlightenment to the barbarities and inequities characteristic of feudal systems of justice.
Frame of reference	One's unique patterning of perceptions and attitudes according to which one evaluates and reacts to events is a frame of reference.
Criminologist	A criminologist is often defined as someone who studies the aetiology of crime, criminal behavior, types of crime, and social, cultural and media reactions to crime.
Positivist criminology	Positivist criminology refers to the second great theoretical movement in modern criminology, which presumes that criminal behavior is caused by factors outside of the individual's control. Its method of analysis is based on the collection of observable scientific facts, and its aim is to uncover, to explain, and to predict the ways in which the observable facts of crime occur.
Rationalization	Rationalization is the process whereby an increasing number of social actions and interactions become based on considerations of efficiency or calculation rather than on motivations derived from custom, tradition, or emotion.
Rational choice	Rational choice theory assumes human behavior is guided by instrumental reason. Accordingly, individuals always choose what they believe to be the best means to achieve their given ends. Thus, they are normally regarded as maximizing utility, the "currency" for everything they cherish (for example: money, a long life, moral standards).
Criminal law	Criminal law (also known as penal law) is the body of statutory and common law that deals with crime and the legal punishment of criminal offenses. There are four theories of criminal justice: punishment, deterrence, incapacitation, and rehabilitation.
Donald Black	Donald Black is author of the 1976 book The Behavior of Law, which has received very favorable reviews, and The Social Structure of Right and Wrong, which applies sociological concepts first explored in The Behavior of Law to subjects other than law, such as Right and Wrong, Crime as Social Control, Conflict Management, art, ideas (as an empirical distributed phenomenon), and God.
Crime rate	Crime rate is a measure of the rate of occurrence of crimes committed in a given area and time. Most commonly, crime rate is given as the number of crimes committed among a given number of persons.
Murder	Murder is the unlawful, premeditated killing of a human being by another. The penalty for murder is usually either life imprisonment, or in jurisdictions with capital punishment, the death penalty.
Felony	The term felony is used for very serious crimes, whereas misdemeanors are considered to be less serious offenses. It is a crime punishable by one or more years of imprisonment.

Go to Cram101.com for the Practice Tests for this Chapter.

Go to **Cram101.com** for the Practice Tests for this Chapter.
And, **NEVER** highlight a book again!

Classical criminology	Criminology based on both free will and determinism and whose chief aim was to deter crime refers to classical criminology. It was part of the humanist reaction during the Enlightenment to the barbarities and inequities characteristic of feudal systems of justice.
Criminology	Criminology refers to the systematic study of crime and the criminal justice system, including the police, courts, and prisons.
Criminal justice	Criminal justice refers to the system used by government to maintain social control, enforce laws, and administer justice. Law enforcement (police), courts, and corrections are the primary agencies charged with these responsibilities.
Crime rate	Crime rate is a measure of the rate of occurrence of crimes committed in a given area and time. Most commonly, crime rate is given as the number of crimes committed among a given number of persons.
Crime	Crime refers to any action that violates criminal laws established by political authority. A crime in a nontechnical sense is an act that violates a very important political or moral command.
Cesare Lombroso	Cesare Lombroso was a historical figure in modern criminology, and the founder of the Italian School of Positivist Criminology. He rejected the established Classical School, which held that crime was a characteristic trait of human nature.
Positivist criminology	Positivist criminology refers to the second great theoretical movement in modern criminology, which presumes that criminal behavior is caused by factors outside of the individual's control. Its method of analysis is based on the collection of observable scientific facts, and its aim is to uncover, to explain, and to predict the ways in which the observable facts of crime occur.
Social contract	The theory of the social contract is based on the assumption that all men live in a state of nature which is not ideal. In order to move away from these conditions men enter into a contract with each other, allowing them to live in peace and unity. The theory of the social contract can be seen as a justification for the formation of the state.
Criminal law	Criminal law (also known as penal law) is the body of statutory and common law that deals with crime and the legal punishment of criminal offenses. There are four theories of criminal justice: punishment, deterrence, incapacitation, and rehabilitation.
Authority	Authority refers to power that is attached to a position that others perceive as legitimate.
Torture	Torture is the infliction of pain intended to break the will of the victim or victims. Any act by which severe pain, whether physical or psychological, is intentionally inflicted on a person as a means of intimidation, deterrence, revenge, punishment, sadism, or to obtain confessions (true or false) for propaganda or political purposes may be called torture.
Punishment	Punishment is the practice of imposing something unpleasant on a subject as a response to some unwanted behavior or disobedience that the subject has displayed.
Consensus	Agreement on basic social values by the members of a group or society is referred to as a consensus.
Foucault	Foucault is known for his critical studies of various social institutions, most notably psychiatry, medicine, parameters of educational timeframes, and the prison system, and also for his work on the history of sexuality.
Penology	Penology comprises penitentiary science: that concerned with the processes devized and adopted for the punishment, repression, and prevention of crime, and the treatment of prisoners.
Government	A government is a body that has the authority to make and the power to enforce laws within a

Go to **Cram101.com** for the Practice Tests for this Chapter.
And, **NEVER** highlight a book again!

	civil, corporate, religious, academic, or other organization or group.
Mannheim	Mannheim was a Jewish Hungarian-born sociologist, influential in the first half of the 20th century and one of the founding fathers of classical sociology. Mannheim rates as a founder of the sociology of knowledge.
Society	A society is a grouping of individuals, which is characterized by common interest and may have distinctive culture and institutions.
Deterrence	Deterrence is a theory from behavioral psychology about preventing or controlling actions or behavior through fear of punishment or retribution. This theory of criminology is shaping the criminal justice system of the United States and various other countries.
Capital punishment	Use of the death penalty to punish offenders is called capital punishment.
Frame of reference	One's unique patterning of perceptions and attitudes according to which one evaluates and reacts to events is a frame of reference.
Crime statistics	Crime statistics attempt to provide a statistical measure of the level, or amount, of crime that is prevalent in societies. Given that crime, by definition, is an illegal activity, every way of measuring it is likely to be inaccurate.
Statistics	Statistics is a mathematical science pertaining to the collection, analysis, interpretation, and presentation of data. It is applicable to a wide variety of academic disciplines, from the physical and social sciences to the humanities; it is also used and misused for making informed decisions in all areas of business and government.
Murder	Murder is the unlawful, premeditated killing of a human being by another. The penalty for murder is usually either life imprisonment, or in jurisdictions with capital punishment, the death penalty.
Rape	Rape is the act of forcing penetrative sexual acts, against another's will through violence, force, threat of injury, or other duress, or where the victim is unable to decline, due to the effects of drugs or alcohol.
Organization	In sociology organization is understood as planned, coordinated and purposeful action of human beings to construct or compile a common tangible or intangible product or service.
Life expectancy	The number of years a newborn in a particular society can expect to live is referred to as a life expectancy.
Population growth	Population growth is change in population over time, and can be quantified as the change in the number of individuals in a population per unit time. The term population growth can technically refer to any species, but almost always refers to humans, and it is often used informally for the more specific demographic term population growth rate , and is often used to refer specifically to the growth of the population of the world.
Adam Smith	Adam Smith, was a Scottish political economist and moral philosopher. His Inquiry into the Nature and Causes of the Wealth of Nations was one of the earliest attempts to study the historical development of industry and commerce in Europe. That work helped to create the modern academic discipline of economics and provided one of the best-known intellectual rationales for free trade, capitalism, and libertarianism.
Malthus	Malthus is best known for his pessimistic, often false, but highly influential views on population growth. It is this theory of Malthus—not some easily dismissed prediction—that has had huge influence on evolutionary theory in both biology (as acknowledged by Darwin and Wallace) and the social sciences (such as Spencer). Malthus's population theory has also profoundly affected the modern day ecological-evolutionary social theory of Gerhard Lenski and Marvin Harris. He can thus be regarded as an element of the canon of socioeconomic

Go to **Cram101.com** for the Practice Tests for this Chapter.

Go to **Cram101.com** for the Practice Tests for this Chapter.
And, **NEVER** highlight a book again!

theory.

Violent crime	A violent crime or crime of violence is a crime in which the offender uses or threatens to use violent force upon the victim. The United States Department of Justice Bureau of Justice Statistics (BJS) counts five categories of crime as violent crimes: murder, rape, robbery, aggravated assault, and simple assault.
Social research	Social research refers to research conducted by social scientists (primarily within sociology and social psychology, but also within other disciplines such as social policy, human geography, political science, social anthropology and education).
Normal distribution	The normal distribution or normal curve, is a probability distribution of great importance in many fields. It is a family of distributions of the same general form, differing in their location and scale parameters: the mean and standard deviation, respectively. The standard normal distribution is the normal distribution with a mean of zero and a variance of one.
Ethnic group	An ethnic group is a human population whose members identify with each other, usually on the basis of a presumed common genealogy or ancestry.
Prejudice	Prejudice is, as the name implies, the process of "pre-judging" something. It implies coming to a judgment on a subject before learning where the preponderance of evidence actually lies, or forming a judgment without direct experience.
Criminaloid	A criminaloid is a person who projects a respectable, upright facade, in an attempt to conceal a criminal personality.
Anthropology	A social science, closely linked to sociology, which concentrates on the study of traditional cultures--particularly hunting and gathering, horticultural societies, and the evolution of the human species is referred to as anthropology.
Insanity	Insanity refers to a legal status indicating that a person cannot be held responsible for his or her actions because of mental illness.
Criminologist	A criminologist is often defined as someone who studies the aetiology of crime, criminal behavior, types of crime, and social, cultural and media reactions to crime.
Variable	A characteristic that varies in value or magnitude along which an object, individual or group may be categorized, such as income or age, is referred to as a variable.
Range	A measure of variability defined as the high score in a distribution minus the low score is referred to as a range.
Mean	In statistics, mean has two related meanings: a)the average in ordinary English, which is also called the arithmetic mean (and is distinguished from the geometric mean or harmonic mean). The average is also called sample mean. b)the expected value of a random variable, which is also called the population mean.

Go to **Cram101.com** for the Practice Tests for this Chapter.
And, **NEVER** highlight a book again!

Biological Determinism	Biological determinism is the hypothesis that biological factors such as an organism's individual genes (as opposed to social or environmental factors) completely determine how a system behaves or changes over time.
Criminology	Criminology refers to the systematic study of crime and the criminal justice system, including the police, courts, and prisons.
Determinism	Determinism is the philosophical proposition that every event, including human cognition and action, is causally determined by an unbroken chain of prior occurrences. No wholly random, spontaneous, mysterious, or miraculous events occur, according to this philosophy.
Crime	Crime refers to any action that violates criminal laws established by political authority. A crime in a nontechnical sense is an act that violates a very important political or moral command.
Cesare Lombroso	Cesare Lombroso was a historical figure in modern criminology, and the founder of the Italian School of Positivist Criminology. He rejected the established Classical School, which held that crime was a characteristic trait of human nature.
Criminologist	A criminologist is often defined as someone who studies the aetiology of crime, criminal behavior, types of crime, and social, cultural and media reactions to crime.
Gramsci	Gramsci was an Italian writer, politician and political theorist. His writings are heavily concerned with the analysis of culture and political leadership and he is notable as a highly original thinker within the Marxist tradition. He opposed a "philosophy of praxis" to materialist dialectics and is renowned for his concept of cultural hegemony as a means of maintaining the state in a capitalist society.
Putnam	Putnam makes a distinction between two kinds of social capital: bonding capital and bridging capital. Bonding occurs when you are socializing with people who are like you: same age, same race, same religion, and so on. But in order to create peaceful societies in a diverse multi-ethnic country, one needs to have a second kind of social capital: bridging.
Anomalies	Scientific findings that either contradict or cannot be explained by a paradigm are referred to as anomalies.
Typology	Typology refers to the classification of observations in terms of their attributes on two or more variables. The classification of newspapers as liberal-urban, liberal-rural, conservative-urban, or conservative-rural would be an example of a typology.
Authority	Authority refers to power that is attached to a position that others perceive as legitimate.
Karl Pearson	Karl Pearson was a major contributor to the early development of statistics, and in 1911 founded the world's first university statistics department at University College London. In 1901, with Weldon and Galton, he founded the journal Biometrika whose object was the development of statistical theory.
Frequency	In statistics the frequency of an event i is the number n_i of times the event occurred in the experiment or the study.
Mannheim	Mannheim was a Jewish Hungarian-born sociologist, influential in the first half of the 20th century and one of the founding fathers of classical sociology. Mannheim rates as a founder of the sociology of knowledge.
Adoption Study	Adoption study refers to a study in which investigators seek to discover whether, in behavior and psychological characteristics, adopted children are more like their adoptive parents, who provided a home environment, or more like their biological parents who contributed their home.
Identical twins	Identical twins occur when a single egg is fertilized to form one zygote (monozygotic) which

Go to **Cram101.com** for the Practice Tests for this Chapter.

Go to **Cram101.com** for the Practice Tests for this Chapter.
And, **NEVER** highlight a book again!

then divides into two separate embryos. This is not considered to be a hereditary trait, but rather an anomaly that occurs in birthing at a rate of about 1:150 births worldwide, regardless of ethnic background. [citation needed]

Dizygotic twins	Dizygotic twins refers to fraternal twins who develop from separate zygotes. Often called fraternal twins.
Abnormal behavior	Actions, thoughts, and feelings that are harmful to the person or to others is referred to as an abnormal behavior.
Labeling	Labeling is defining or describing a person in terms of his or her behavior. The term is often used in sociology to describe human interaction, control and identification of deviant behavior.
Glaser	Glaser, American sociologist and one of the founders of the grounded theory methodology. In 1999 Glaser founded the non-profit web based organization Grounded Theory Institute.
Substance abuse	Substance abuse refers to the overindulgence in and dependence on a psychoactive leading to effects that are detrimental to the individual's physical health or mental health, or the welfare of others.
Gender	Gender refers to socially defined behavior regarded as appropriate for the members of each
Reliability	Reliability refers to the degree to which a measurement instrument gives the same results with repeated measurements.
Pilot study	A pilot study is a precursor to a full-scale study. Usually conducted with a smaller sample size than the full study, a pilot study is generally intended to test experimental procedures and to obtain information useful for conducting power calculations.
Socioeconomic status	An overall rank based on characteristics such as education and occupation, used to describe people's positions in stratification systems is referred to as socioeconomic status.
Personality disorder	Personality disorder refers to a mental disorder characterized by a set of inflexible, maladaptive personality traits that keep a person from functioning properly in society.
Social class	A category of people who occupy a similar position in relation to the means through which goods and services are produced in a society is a social class.
Criminal law	Criminal law (also known as penal law) is the body of statutory and common law that deals with crime and the legal punishment of criminal offenses. There are four theories of criminal justice: punishment, deterrence, incapacitation, and rehabilitation.
Etiology	Etiology is the study of causation. It is derived from the Greek meaning 'concerned with causes', and so can refer to myths as well as to medical and philosophical theories.
Cohort	A cohort is a group of subjects, most often humans from a given population, defined by experiencing an event (typically birth) in a particular time span.
Statistical significance	The condition that exists when the probability that the observed findings are due to chance is very low is a statistical significance.
Dopamine	Dopamine refers to a neurotransmitter that functions in the parts of the brain that control emotions and bodily movement.
Wilson	In The Declining Significance of Race: Blacks and Changing American Institutions Wilson argues that the significance of race is waning, and an African-American's class is comparatively more important in determining his or her life chances.
Juvenile delinquency	Juvenile delinquency refers to antisocial or criminal acts performed by minors. It is an important social issue because juveniles are capable of committing serious crimes, but most legal systems prescribe specific procedures and punishments for dealing with such crimes.

Go to **Cram101.com** for the Practice Tests for this Chapter.

Go to **Cram101.com** for the Practice Tests for this Chapter.
And, **NEVER** highlight a book again!

Criminal justice	Criminal justice refers to the system used by government to maintain social control, enforce laws, and administer justice. Law enforcement (police), courts, and corrections are the primary agencies charged with these responsibilities.
Dysfunction	Dysfunction refers to an institution's negative impact on the sociocultural system.
Punishment	Punishment is the practice of imposing something unpleasant on a subject as a response to some unwanted behavior or disobedience that the subject has displayed.
Socialization	Socialization refers to the lifelong processes through which humans develop an awareness of social norms and values, and achieve a distinct sense of self.
Reinforcement	A stimulus that follows a response and increases the frequency of the response is a reinforcement.
Inner city	The areas composing the central neighborhoods of industrial cities which are subject to dilapidation and decay, with the more affluent residents having moved to outlying area is an inner city.
Cocaine	Cocaine is a crystalline tropane alkaloid that is obtained from the leaves of the coca plant. It is a stimulant of the central nervous system and an appetite suppressant, creating what has been described as a euphoric sense of happiness and increased energy.
Causal Relationship	A relationship in which one state of affairs is brought about by another is defined as a causal relationship.
Intake	Intake refers to process during which a juvenile referral is received and a decision is made to file a petition in juvenile court to release the juvenile, to place the juvenile under supervision, or to refer the juvenile elsewhere.
Validity	The degree to which a measurement instrument measures what it is intended to measure is referred to as validity.
Disability	A physical or health condition that stigmatizes or causes discrimination, is referred to as a disability.
Consciousness	The awareness of the senzations, thoughts, and feelings being experienced at a given moment is referred to as consciousness.
Child abuse	Child abuse refers to not only physical assaults on a child but also malnourishment, abandonment, neglect, emotional abuse and sexual abuse.
Violent crime	A violent crime or crime of violence is a crime in which the offender uses or threatens to use violent force upon the victim. The United States Department of Justice Bureau of Justice Statistics (BJS) counts five categories of crime as violent crimes: murder, rape, robbery, aggravated assault, and simple assault.

Go to **Cram101.com** for the Practice Tests for this Chapter.
And, **NEVER** highlight a book again!

Crime	Crime refers to any action that violates criminal laws established by political authority. A crime in a nontechnical sense is an act that violates a very important political or moral command.
Putnam	Putnam makes a distinction between two kinds of social capital: bonding capital and bridging capital. Bonding occurs when you are socializing with people who are like you: same age, same race, same religion, and so on. But in order to create peaceful societies in a diverse multi-ethnic country, one needs to have a second kind of social capital: bridging.
DuBois	DuBois was the most prominent intellectual leader and political activist on behalf of African Americans in the first half of the twentieth century. A contemporary of Booker T. Washington, the two carried on a dialogue about segregation and political disenfranchisement. He was labeled "The Father of Pan-Africanism."
Criminology	Criminology refers to the systematic study of crime and the criminal justice system, including the police, courts, and prisons.
Mental age	Mental age is a controversial concept in psychometrics. It is an intelligence test score, expressed as the chronological age for which a given level of performance is average or typical.
Standard deviation	In probability and statistics, the standard deviation of a probability distribution, random variable, or population or multiset of values is defined as the square root of the variance.
Mean	In statistics, mean has two related meanings: a)the average in ordinary English, which is also called the arithmetic mean (and is distinguished from the geometric mean or harmonic mean). The average is also called sample mean. b)the expected value of a random variable, which is also called the population mean.
Adaptation	Adaptation refers to the ability of a sociocultural system to change with the demands of a changing physical or social environment.
Social role	A social role is a set of connected behaviors, rights and obligations as conceptualized by actors in a social situation. It is mostly defined as an expected behavior in a given individual social status and social position.
Median	The number that falls halfway in a range of numbers, or the score below which are half the scores and above which are the other half is a median.
Government	A government is a body that has the authority to make and the power to enforce laws within a civil, corporate, religious, academic, or other organization or group.
Minority group	A minority group or subordinate group is a sociological group that does not constitute a politically dominant plurality of the total population of a given society.
Industrialized societies	Strongly developed nation-states in which the majority of the population work in factories or offices rather than in agriculture, and most people live in urban areas are referred to as industrialized societies.
Society	A society is a grouping of individuals, which is characterized by common interest and may have distinctive culture and institutions.
Juvenile justice system	The segment of the justice system including law enforcement officers, the courts, and correctional agencies, designed to treat youthful offenders is referred to as the juvenile justice system.
Educational attainment	Educational attainment is a term commonly used by statisticans to refer to the highest degree of education an individual has completed.
Social class	A category of people who occupy a similar position in relation to the means through which goods and services are produced in a society is a social class.

Go to **Cram101.com** for the Practice Tests for this Chapter.

Go to **Cram101.com** for the Practice Tests for this Chapter.
And, **NEVER** highlight a book again!

Official delinquency	Official delinquency refers to delinquent acts that result in arrest by local police. These are included in the FBI's arrest data.
Criminal justice	Criminal justice refers to the system used by government to maintain social control, enforce laws, and administer justice. Law enforcement (police), courts, and corrections are the primary agencies charged with these responsibilities.
Social policy	Social policy relates to guidelines for the changing, maintenance or creation of living conditions that are conducive to human welfare. Thus social policy is that part of public policy that has to do with social issues such as public access to social programs.
Statistics	Statistics is a mathematical science pertaining to the collection, analysis, interpretation, and presentation of data. It is applicable to a wide variety of academic disciplines, from the physical and social sciences to the humanities; it is also used and misused for making informed decisions in all areas of business and government.
Cohort	A cohort is a group of subjects, most often humans from a given population, defined by experiencing an event (typically birth) in a particular time span.
Group process	In organizational development (OD), or group dynamics, the phrase group process refers to the understanding of the behavior of people in groups, such as task groups that are trying to solve a problem or make a decision.
Gang	A gang is a group of individuals who share a common identity and, in current usage, engage in illegal activities. Historically the term referred to both criminal groups and ordinary groups of friends.
Bias	A bias is a prejudice in a general or specific sense, usually in the sense for having a preference to one particular point of view or ideological perspective.
Differential Association	In criminology, Differential Association is a theory developed by Edwin Sutherland proposing that through interaction with others, individuals learn the values, attitudes, techniques, and motives for criminal behavior.
Conflict theory	Conflict theory or conflict perspective refers to a theory that conflict is normal and that the task is not to eliminate conflict but to learn to control it so that it becomes constructive.
Labeling	Labeling is defining or describing a person in terms of his or her behavior. The term is often used in sociology to describe human interaction, control and identification of deviant behavior.
Social Control Theory	In criminology, Social Control Theory as represented in the work of Travis Hirschi fits into the Positivist School, Neo-Classical School, and, later, Right Realism. It proposes that exploiting the process of socialization and social learning builds self-control and reduces the inclination to indulge in behavior recognized as antisocial.
Social control	A social mechanism that regulates individual and group behavior through sanctions and rewards is a social control.
Control theory	A theory that views crime as the outcome of an imbalance between impulses toward criminal activity and controls that deter it is referred to as control theory. Control theorists hold that criminals are rational beings who will act to maximize their own reward.
Attitude	Attitude refers to an enduring mental representation of a person, place, or thing that evokes an emotional response and related behavior.
Family therapy	Family therapy is a branch of psychotherapy that works with families and couples in intimate relationships to nurture change and development. It tends to view these in terms of the systems of interaction between family members.

21

Wilson	In The Declining Significance of Race: Blacks and Changing American Institutions Wilson argues that the significance of race is waning, and an African-American's class is comparatively more important in determining his or her life chances.
Juvenile delinquency	Juvenile delinquency refers to antisocial or criminal acts performed by minors. It is an important social issue because juveniles are capable of committing serious crimes, but most legal systems prescribe specific procedures and punishments for dealing with such crimes.
Cultural bias	Cultural bias refers to a factor that provides an advantage for test takers from certain cultural or ethnic backgrounds, such as using test items that are based on middle-class culture in the United States.
Control group	A group of people in an experiment who are not exposed to the experimental stimulus under study are referred to as a control group.
Minnesota multiphasic personality inventory	The Minnesota Multiphasic Personality Inventory is the most frequently used personality test in the mental health fields. This assessment, or test, was designed to help identify personal, social, and behavioral problems in psychiatric patients.
Personality disorder	Personality disorder refers to a mental disorder characterized by a set of inflexible, maladaptive personality traits that keep a person from functioning properly in society.
Social problem	A social condition that is perceived as having harmful effects is a social problem. Opinions about whether a condition is a social problem vary among groups and depend upon how and by whom the condition is defined and perceived in society.
Recidivism	The probability that those incarcerated and then released are likely to return to prison for the commission of new crimes is referred to as recidivism.
Violent crime	A violent crime or crime of violence is a crime in which the offender uses or threatens to use violent force upon the victim. The United States Department of Justice Bureau of Justice Statistics (BJS) counts five categories of crime as violent crimes: murder, rape, robbery, aggravated assault, and simple assault.
Frequency	In statistics the frequency of an event i is the number n_i of times the event occurred in the experiment or the study.
Crime prevention	Crime prevention is a term describing techniques used in reducing victimization as well as deterring crime and criminals. It is applied specifically to efforts made by governments to reduce crime and law enforcement and criminal justice.
Subculture	A group within the broader society that has values, norms and lifestyle distinct from those of the majority, is referred to as a subculture.
Mass media	Mass media refers to forms of communication designed to reach a vast audience without any personal contact between the senders and receivers.
Interpersonal relationship	An interpersonal relationship is a social association, connection, or affiliation between two or more people. They vary in differing levels of intimacy and sharing, implying the discovery or establishment of common ground, and may be centered around something(s) shared in common.
Mores	Mores are strongly held norms or customs. These derive from the established practices of a society rather than its written laws.
Entitlement	The feeling that one has a right to certain privileges and that specific rewards should be forthcoming by virtue of what they have done or who they are is an entitlement.
Analogy	Analogy is either the cognitive process of transferring or giving information from a particular subject to another particular subject, or a linguistic expression corresponding to such a process. In a narrower sense, analogy is an inference or an argument from a particular

Go to **Cram101.com** for the Practice Tests for this Chapter.

Go to **Cram101.com** for the Practice Tests for this Chapter.
And, **NEVER** highlight a book again!

to another particular, as opposed to deduction, induction, and abduction, where at least one of the premises or the conclusion is general.

Criminologist   A criminologist is often defined as someone who studies the aetiology of crime, criminal behavior, types of crime, and social, cultural and media reactions to crime.

Go to **Cram101.com** for the Practice Tests for this Chapter.
And, **NEVER** highlight a book again!

Empirical study	An empirical study in social sciences is when the research ends are based on evidence and not just theory. This is done to comply with the scientific method that asserts the objective discovery of knowledge based on verifiable facts of evidence.
Crime	Crime refers to any action that violates criminal laws established by political authority. A crime in a nontechnical sense is an act that violates a very important political or moral command.
Crime rate	Crime rate is a measure of the rate of occurrence of crimes committed in a given area and time. Most commonly, crime rate is given as the number of crimes committed among a given number of persons.
Unemployment rate	In economics, one who is willing to work at a prevailing wage rate yet is unable to find a paying job is considered to be unemployed. The unemployment rate is the number of unemployed workers divided by the total civilian labor force, which includes both the unemployed and those with jobs (all those willing and able to work for pay).
Contradiction	Marx's term to refer to mutually antagonistic tendencies within institutions or the broader society such as those between profit and competition within capitalism is referred to as a contradiction.
Violent crime	A violent crime or crime of violence is a crime in which the offender uses or threatens to use violent force upon the victim. The United States Department of Justice Bureau of Justice Statistics (BJS) counts five categories of crime as violent crimes: murder, rape, robbery, aggravated assault, and simple assault.
Depression	In the field of psychiatry, the word depression can also have this meaning of low mood but more specifically refers to a mental illness when it has reached a severity and duration to warrant a diagnosis, whether there is an obvious situational cause or not.
Criminology	Criminology refers to the systematic study of crime and the criminal justice system, including the police, courts, and prisons.
Criminal justice	Criminal justice refers to the system used by government to maintain social control, enforce laws, and administer justice. Law enforcement (police), courts, and corrections are the primary agencies charged with these responsibilities.
Wright	Wright is an American sociologist. His work is concerned mainly with the study of social classes, and in particular with the task of providing an update to the Marxist concept of class. Wright has stressed the importance of the control of the means of production in defining 'class', while at the same trying to account for the situation of skilled employees, taking inspiration from Weberian accounts of authority.
Positive relationship	A statistical relationship in which high scores on one variable are related to high scores on another variable, is referred to as a direct or positive relationship.
Median	The number that falls halfway in a range of numbers, or the score below which are half the scores and above which are the other half is a median.
Social forces	Social forces are the typical basic drives, or motives, which lead to the fundamental types of association and group relationship.
Subculture	A group within the broader society that has values, norms and lifestyle distinct from those of the majority, is referred to as a subculture.
Punishment	Punishment is the practice of imposing something unpleasant on a subject as a response to some unwanted behavior or disobedience that the subject has displayed.
Population density	Population density refers to the number of people per unit of area or unit volume.

Go to **Cram101.com** for the Practice Tests for this Chapter.
And, **NEVER** highlight a book again!

Social structure	The term social structure, used in a general sense, refers to entities or groups in definite relation to each other, to relatively enduring patterns of behavior and relationship within social systems, or to social institutions and norms becoming embedded into social systems in such a way that they shape the behavior of actors within those social systems.
Victimization surveys	Victimization surveys attempts to bypass the underreporting problem by going directly to the victims. The National Crime Victimization Survey (NCVS) is conducted by the U.S. Bureau of the Census in cooperation with the Bureau of Justice Statistics and the U.S. Department of Justice. The NCVS polls over 50,000 households, totaling over 100,000 individuals, in the United States annually using a multistage sample of housing units. Individuals over 12 years old in selected households are interviewed every six months for about three years.
Social problem	A social condition that is perceived as having harmful effects is a social problem. Opinions about whether a condition is a social problem vary among groups and depend upon how and by whom the condition is defined and perceived in society.
Statistics	Statistics is a mathematical science pertaining to the collection, analysis, interpretation, and presentation of data. It is applicable to a wide variety of academic disciplines, from the physical and social sciences to the humanities; it is also used and misused for making informed decisions in all areas of business and government.
Glaser	Glaser, American sociologist and one of the founders of the grounded theory methodology. In 1999 Glaser founded the non-profit web based organization Grounded Theory Institute.
Social issue	Social issue refers to matters that can be explained only by factors outside an individual's control and immediate social environment. They usually concern more than a single individual and affect many individuals in a society.
Juvenile delinquency	Juvenile delinquency refers to antisocial or criminal acts performed by minors. It is an important social issue because juveniles are capable of committing serious crimes, but most legal systems prescribe specific procedures and punishments for dealing with such crimes.
Political economy	The social arrangements through which political and economic institutions support each other is a political economy.
Direct relationship	In mathematics and statistics, a positive or direct relationship is a relationship between two variables in which they both increase or decrease in conjunction.
Political crime	A term used to describe illegal or unethical acts involving the usurpation of power by government officials or illegal or unethical acts perpetrated against the government by outsiders seeking to make a political statement or undermine the government, is referred to as a political crime.
Demographics	The analysis of data used by advertizing agencies to target an audience by sex, age, income level, marital status, geographic location, and occupation are referred to as demographics.
Social research	Social research refers to research conducted by social scientists (primarily within sociology and social psychology, but also within other disciplines such as social policy, human geography, political science, social anthropology and education).
Public policy	Public policy is a course of action or inaction chosen by public authorities to address a problem. Public policy is expressed in the body of laws, regulations, decisions and actions of government.
Wilson	In The Declining Significance of Race: Blacks and Changing American Institutions Wilson argues that the significance of race is waning, and an African-American's class is comparatively more important in determining his or her life chances.
Criminal law	Criminal law (also known as penal law) is the body of statutory and common law that deals with crime and the legal punishment of criminal offenses. There are four theories of criminal

Go to **Cram101.com** for the Practice Tests for this Chapter.
And, **NEVER** highlight a book again!

	justice: punishment, deterrence, incapacitation, and rehabilitation.
Government	A government is a body that has the authority to make and the power to enforce laws within a civil, corporate, religious, academic, or other organization or group.
Negative relationship	A relationship in which high scores on one variable are related to low scores on another is a negative relationship.
Variable	A characteristic that varies in value or magnitude along which an object, individual or group may be categorized, such as income or age, is referred to as a variable.
Robbery	The unlawful taking of, or the attempt to take something of value from another person or persons by using violence or the threat of violence, is referred to as a robbery.
Rape	Rape is the act of forcing penetrative sexual acts, against another's will through violence, force, threat of injury, or other duress, or where the victim is unable to decline, due to the effects of drugs or alcohol.
Burglary	Burglary – also called breaking and entering or house breaking – is a crime related to theft. It typically involves someone breaking into a house with an intent to commit a crime.
Social influence	Social influence is when the actions or thoughts of individual(s) are changed by other individual(s). Examples of social influence can be seen in socialization and peer pressure. This is the effect of other people on a person's behavior.
Social progress	Social progress is defined as a progress of society, which makes the society better in the general view of its members, or unintentionally worse, with or without its members realizing
Larceny	Larceny is the trespassory taking and asportation of the (tangible) personal property of another with the intent to deprive him or her of it permanently.
Community	Community refers to a group of people who share a common sense of identity and interact with one another on a sustained basis.
Neighborhood	A neighborhood is a geographically localized community located within a larger city, town or suburb. Traditionally, a neighborhood is small enough that the neighbors are all able to know each other.
Social control	A social mechanism that regulates individual and group behavior through sanctions and rewards is a social control.
Causality	One factor has an effect on or produces a change in another factor is referred to as causality.
Mean	In statistics, mean has two related meanings: a)the average in ordinary English, which is also called the arithmetic mean (and is distinguished from the geometric mean or harmonic mean). The average is also called sample mean. b)the expected value of a random variable, which is also called the population mean.
Social stigma	Social stigma refers to severe social disapproval of personal characteristics that is against cultural norms. Social stigma often leads to marginalization.
Human capital	Human capital is a way of defining and categorizing peoples' skills and abilities as used in employment and as they otherwise contribute to the economy. Many early economic theories refer to it simply as labor, one of three factors of production, and consider it to be a commodity.
Metropolitan area	A metropolitan area is a large population center consisting of a large city and its adjacent zone of influence, or of several neighboring cities or towns and adjoining areas, with one or more large cities serving as its hub or hubs.
Baseline	Measure of a particular behavior or process taken before the introduction of the independent

Go to **Cram101.com** for the Practice Tests for this Chapter.
And, **NEVER** highlight a book again!

	variable or treatment is referred to as a baseline.
Gini coefficient	The Gini coefficient is a measure of inequality of a distribution. It is defined as a ratio with values between 0 and 1: the numerator is the area between the Lorenz curve of the distribution and the uniform (perfect) distribution line; the denominator is the area under the uniform distribution line.
Society	A society is a grouping of individuals, which is characterized by common interest and may have distinctive culture and institutions.
Gini	Gini was an Italian statistician, demographer and sociologist who developed the Gini coefficient, a measure of the income inequality in a society. Gini was also a leading fascist theorist and ideologue who wrote The Scientific Basis of Fascism in 1927.
Material good	In economics and philosophy, a material good is a good that can be purchased or sold and from which one receives non-spiritual pleasure.
Deviant behavior	Deviant behavior is behavior that is a recognized violation of social norms. Formal and informal social controls attempt to prevent and minimize deviance. One such control is through the medicalization of deviance.
Social capital	Social capital is defined as the advantage created by a person's location in a structure of relationships. It explains how some people gain more success in a particular setting through their superior connections to other people. There are in fact a variety of inter-related definitions of this term, which has been described as "something of a cure-all" (Portes, 1998) for all the problems afflicting communities and societies today.
Underclass	A class of individuals in mature industrial societies situated at the bottom of the class system who have been systematically excluded from participation in economic life are the underclass.
Family disruption	Family disruption refers to the behaviors associated with altering or terminating family and pseudo-family units; separation, annulment, divorce, disownment, death, etc.

Go to **Cram101.com** for the Practice Tests for this Chapter.
And, **NEVER** highlight a book again!

Durkheim	Durkheim sought to create one of the first scientific approaches to social phenomena. Along with Herbert Spencer, Durkheim was one of the first people to explain the existence and quality of different parts of a society by reference to what function they served in keeping the society healthy and balanced—a position that would come to be known as functionalism.
Crime	Crime refers to any action that violates criminal laws established by political authority. A crime in a nontechnical sense is an act that violates a very important political or moral command.
Norm	In sociology, a norm, or social norm, is a rule that is socially enforced. Social sanctioning is what distinguishes norms from other cultural products such as meaning and values.
Modernization	The process of general social change brought about by the transition from an agrarian to an industrial mode of production, is referred to as modernization.
Social change	Social change refers to alteration in social structures or culture over time.
Society	A society is a grouping of individuals, which is characterized by common interest and may have distinctive culture and institutions.
Anomie	Durkheim's designation for a condition in which social control becomes ineffective as a result of the loss of shared values and a sense of purpose in society is defined as anomie.
Criminology	Criminology refers to the systematic study of crime and the criminal justice system, including the police, courts, and prisons.
Juvenile delinquency	Juvenile delinquency refers to antisocial or criminal acts performed by minors. It is an important social issue because juveniles are capable of committing serious crimes, but most legal systems prescribe specific procedures and punishments for dealing with such crimes.
Industrializtion	Industrialization is a process of social and economic change whereby a human society is transformed from a pre-industrial (an economy where the amount of capital accumulated is low) to an industrial state
Auguste Comte	Auguste Comte(1798-1857) was a French positivist thinker and came up with the term of sociology to name the new science made by Saint-Simon.
Comte	Comte coined the term "sociology." He is remembered for being the first to apply the scientific method to the social world. He coined the word "altruism" to refer to what he believed to be a moral obligations of individuals to serve others and place their interests above one's own. He opposed the idea of individual rights, maintaining that they were not consistent with this supposed ethical obligation.
Solidarity	Solidarity in sociology refers to the feeling or condition of unity based on common goals, interests, and sympathies among a group's members. Solidarity refers to the ties in a society - social relations - that bind people to one another.
Division of labor	Division of labor is the specialisation of cooperative labor in specific, circumscribed tasks and roles, intended to increase efficiency of output.
Social group	A group that consists of two or more people who interact frequently and share a common identity and a feeling of interdependence, is referred to as a social group.
Clan	A clan is a group of people united by kinship and descent, which is defined by perceived descent from a common ancestor found in many pre-industrial societies.
Restitution	The law of restitution is the law of gains-based recovery. When a court orders restitution it orders the defendant to give up his gains to the claimant.
Collective conscience	Durkheim's term for the moral consensus of a society that is violated by deviant acts is referred to as collective conscience.

35

Sanction	A punishment for nonconformity that reinforces socially approved forms of behavior is a sanction.
Consciousness	The awareness of the senzations, thoughts, and feelings being experienced at a given moment is referred to as consciousness.
Punishment	Punishment is the practice of imposing something unpleasant on a subject as a response to some unwanted behavior or disobedience that the subject has displayed.
Deterrence	Deterrence is a theory from behavioral psychology about preventing or controlling actions or behavior through fear of punishment or retribution. This theory of criminology is shaping the criminal justice system of the United States and various other countries.
Social structure	The term social structure, used in a general sense, refers to entities or groups in definite relation to each other, to relatively enduring patterns of behavior and relationship within social systems, or to social institutions and norms becoming embedded into social systems in such a way that they shape the behavior of actors within those social systems.
Criminal law	Criminal law (also known as penal law) is the body of statutory and common law that deals with crime and the legal punishment of criminal offenses. There are four theories of criminal justice: punishment, deterrence, incapacitation, and rehabilitation.
Conformity	Conformity is the act of consciously maintaining a certain degree of similarity (in clothing, manners, behaviors, etc.) to those in your general social circles, to those in authority, or to the general status quo. Usually, conformity implies a tendency to submit to others in thought and behavior other than simply clothing choice.
Public health	Public health is concerned with threats to the overall health of a community based on population health analysis.
Civil Rights Movement	Historically, the civil rights movement was a concentrated period of time around the world of approximately one generation (1954-1980) wherein there was much worldwide civil unrest and popular rebellion.
Civil rights	Civil rights are the protections and privileges of personal liberty given to all citizens by law. Civil rights are rights that are bestowed by nations on those within their territorial boundaries.
Crime rate	Crime rate is a measure of the rate of occurrence of crimes committed in a given area and time. Most commonly, crime rate is given as the number of crimes committed among a given number of persons.
Alienation	In sociology and critical social theory, alienation refers to the individual's estrangement from traditional community and others in general.
Deviant behavior	Deviant behavior is behavior that is a recognized violation of social norms. Formal and informal social controls attempt to prevent and minimize deviance. One such control is through the medicalization of deviance.
Depression	In the field of psychiatry, the word depression can also have this meaning of low mood but more specifically refers to a mental illness when it has reached a severity and duration to warrant a diagnosis, whether there is an obvious situational cause or not.
Authority	Authority refers to power that is attached to a position that others perceive as legitimate.
Government	A government is a body that has the authority to make and the power to enforce laws within a civil, corporate, religious, academic, or other organization or group.
Community	Community refers to a group of people who share a common sense of identity and interact with one another on a sustained basis.

Go to **Cram101.com** for the Practice Tests for this Chapter.

Go to **Cram101.com** for the Practice Tests for this Chapter.
And, **NEVER** highlight a book again!

Research methods	The diverse strategies used to gather empirical material in a systematic way are research methods.
Social control	A social mechanism that regulates individual and group behavior through sanctions and rewards is a social control.
Social problem	A social condition that is perceived as having harmful effects is a social problem. Opinions about whether a condition is a social problem vary among groups and depend upon how and by whom the condition is defined and perceived in society.
Cooley	Cooley was an American sociologist whose concept of the "looking glass self" is undoubtedly his most famous, and is known and accepted by most psychologists and sociologists today. It expanded William James's idea of self to include the capacity of reflection on its own behavior. Other people's views build, change and maintain our self-image; thus, there is an interaction between how we see ourselves and how others see us.
Industrialized societies	Strongly developed nation-states in which the majority of the population work in factories or offices rather than in agriculture, and most people live in urban areas are referred to as industrialized societies.
Tolerance	Tolerance is a recent political term used within debates in areas of social, cultural and religious context, as an emphatic antithesis to discrimination, as such may advocate persecution. Its usage came about as a more widely acceptable alternative to "acceptance", the usage of which had been widely derided, as certain cases would not be considered by common society as acceptable.
Case Study	Case study refers to a research design that focuses on a single example rather than a representative sample.
Collective behavior	Collective behavior refers to the relatively unstructured behavior of people in crowds and masses, which is often a voluntary, spontaneous, activity that is engaged in by a large number of people and typically violates dominant group norms and values.
Normlessness	Emile Durkheim described anomie which is state of relative normlessness or a state in which norms have been eroded.
Elite	The elite is a relatively small dominant group within a larger society, which enjoys a privileged status which is upheld by individuals of lower social status within the structure of a group.
Control theory	A theory that views crime as the outcome of an imbalance between impulses toward criminal activity and controls that deter it is referred to as control theory. Control theorists hold that criminals are rational beings who will act to maximize their own reward.
Organization	In sociology organization is understood as planned, coordinated and purposeful action of human beings to construct or compile a common tangible or intangible product or service.
Foucault	Foucault is known for his critical studies of various social institutions, most notably psychiatry, medicine, parameters of educational timeframes, and the prison system, and also for his work on the history of sexuality.
Industrial revolution	Industrial Revolution refers to the massive social, economic, and technological change in 18th and 19th century Great Britian. It commenced with the advent of the steam engine. Spread throughout Western Europe and North America in the 19th century.
Violent crime	A violent crime or crime of violence is a crime in which the offender uses or threatens to use violent force upon the victim. The United States Department of Justice Bureau of Justice Statistics (BJS) counts five categories of crime as violent crimes: murder, rape, robbery, aggravated assault, and simple assault.

Go to **Cram101.com** for the Practice Tests for this Chapter.

Go to **Cram101.com** for the Practice Tests for this Chapter.
And, **NEVER** highlight a book again!

Statistics	Statistics is a mathematical science pertaining to the collection, analysis, interpretation, and presentation of data. It is applicable to a wide variety of academic disciplines, from the physical and social sciences to the humanities; it is also used and misused for making informed decisions in all areas of business and government.
Robbery	The unlawful taking of, or the attempt to take something of value from another person or persons by using violence or the threat of violence, is referred to as a robbery.
Criminologist	A criminologist is often defined as someone who studies the aetiology of crime, criminal behavior, types of crime, and social, cultural and media reactions to crime.
Urbanization	Urbanization is the increase over time in the population of cities in relation to the region's rural population. Urbanization has intense effects on the ecology of a region and on its economy.
Economic development	Economic development is the development of the economic wealth of countries or regions for the well-being of their inhabitants. Economic development is a sustainable increase in living standards that implies increased per capita income, better education and health as well as environmental protection.
Collective violence	Collective violence is the use of violence by members of a group against another group or set of individuals to achieve a social objective.
Urbanism	Urbanism is the study of cities - their economic, political, social and cultural environment, and the imprint of all these forces on the built environment.
Berger	Berger is perhaps best known for his view that social reality is a form of consciousness. Central to his work is the relationship between society and the individual. In his book The Social Construction of Reality Berger develops a sociological theory: 'Society as Objective Reality and as Subjective Reality'. His analysis of society as subjective reality describes the process by which an individual's conception of reality is produced by his or her interaction with social structures.
Age Structure	The relative proportions of different age categories in a population is referred to as an age structure. The distribution of a population according to age, usually by 5-year age groups.
Variable	A characteristic that varies in value or magnitude along which an object, individual or group may be categorized, such as income or age, is referred to as a variable.
Dominance	In animal colonies, a condition established by one animal over another by prevailing in an aggressive encounter between the two, is referred to as dominance.
Criminal justice	Criminal justice refers to the system used by government to maintain social control, enforce laws, and administer justice. Law enforcement (police), courts, and corrections are the primary agencies charged with these responsibilities.
Criminalization	Criminalization refers to the process whereby criminal law is selectively applied to social behavior. It involves the enactment of legislation that outlaws certain types of behavior and provides for surveillance and policing of that behavior and whether or not the behavior is detected.
Social forces	Social forces are the typical basic drives, or motives, which lead to the fundamental types of association and group relationship.
Developmental process	Developmental process refers to at different stages of the life course a variety of factors can influence behavior; factors influential at one stage of life may not be significant at a later stage.
Social equality	Social equality is a social state of affairs in which certain different people have the same status in a certain respect, at the very least in voting rights, freedom of speech and

Go to **Cram101.com** for the Practice Tests for this Chapter.

Go to **Cram101.com** for the Practice Tests for this Chapter.
And, **NEVER** highlight a book again!

assembly, the extent of property rights as well as the access to education, health care and other social securities.

Go to **Cram101.com** for the Practice Tests for this Chapter.
And, **NEVER** highlight a book again!

Chicago school	In sociology and, later, criminology, the Chicago School (sometimes described as the Ecological School) refers to the first major body of works emerging during the 1920s and 1930s specializing in urban sociology, and the research into the urban environment by combining theory and ethnographic fieldwork in Chicago, now applied elsewhere.
Human ecology	Human ecology is an academic discipline that deals with the relationship between humans and their natural, social and created environments. Human ecology investigates how humans and human societies interact with nature and with their environment.
Community	Community refers to a group of people who share a common sense of identity and interact with one another on a sustained basis.
Criminology	Criminology refers to the systematic study of crime and the criminal justice system, including the police, courts, and prisons.
Government	A government is a body that has the authority to make and the power to enforce laws within a civil, corporate, religious, academic, or other organization or group.
Organization	In sociology organization is understood as planned, coordinated and purposeful action of human beings to construct or compile a common tangible or intangible product or service.
Society	A society is a grouping of individuals, which is characterized by common interest and may have distinctive culture and institutions.
Neighborhood	A neighborhood is a geographically localized community located within a larger city, town or suburb. Traditionally, a neighborhood is small enough that the neighbors are all able to know each other.
Dominance	In animal colonies, a condition established by one animal over another by prevailing in an aggressive encounter between the two, is referred to as dominance.
Ernest Burgess	Burgess was an urban sociologist. His groundbreaking social ecology research, in conjunction with his colleague, Robert E. Park, provided the foundation for The Chicago School. In The City , they conceptualized the city into the concentric zones, including the central business district, transitional (industrial, deteriorating housing, ...), working class residential (tenements), residential, and commuter/suburban zones.
Juvenile delinquency	Juvenile delinquency refers to antisocial or criminal acts performed by minors. It is an important social issue because juveniles are capable of committing serious crimes, but most legal systems prescribe specific procedures and punishments for dealing with such crimes.
Crime	Crime refers to any action that violates criminal laws established by political authority. A crime in a nontechnical sense is an act that violates a very important political or moral command.
Probation	Nonpunitive, legal disposition of juveniles emphasizing community treatment in which the juvenile is closely supervized by an officer of the court and must adhere to a strict set of rules to avoid incarceration is probation.
Criminologist	A criminologist is often defined as someone who studies the aetiology of crime, criminal behavior, types of crime, and social, cultural and media reactions to crime.
Life history	Life history refers to a variety of methods and techniques that are used for conducting qualitative interviews. The method was first used when interviewing indigenous peoples of the Americas.
Median	The number that falls halfway in a range of numbers, or the score below which are half the scores and above which are the other half is a median.
Insanity	Insanity refers to a legal status indicating that a person cannot be held responsible for his or her actions because of mental illness.

Go to **Cram101.com** for the Practice Tests for this Chapter.
And, **NEVER** highlight a book again!

Population composition	Population composition refers to the biological and social characteristics of a population. Age and sex composition are the most often considered aspects of population composition, although socio-economic characteristics, such as household income levels, can also be considered compositional.
Public opinion	Public opinion is the aggregate of individual attitudes or beliefs held by the adult population.
Social control	A social mechanism that regulates individual and group behavior through sanctions and rewards is a social control.
Shoplifting	Shoplifting (also known as retail theft) is theft of merchandise for sale in a shop, store, or other retail establishment, by an ostensible patron. It is one of the most common crimes for police and courts.
Social problem	A social condition that is perceived as having harmful effects is a social problem. Opinions about whether a condition is a social problem vary among groups and depend upon how and by whom the condition is defined and perceived in society.
Mean	In statistics, mean has two related meanings: a)the average in ordinary English, which is also called the arithmetic mean (and is distinguished from the geometric mean or harmonic mean). The average is also called sample mean. b)the expected value of a random variable, which is also called the population mean.
Criminal justice	Criminal justice refers to the system used by government to maintain social control, enforce laws, and administer justice. Law enforcement (police), courts, and corrections are the primary agencies charged with these responsibilities.
Social disorganization	Social disorganization refers to a structural condition of society caused by rapid change in social institutions, norms, and values.
Chicago Area Project	Chicago Area Project is a Juvenile delinquency prevention association based in Chicago, Illinois, United States. The association has been acting since early 20th century and is considered to be America's first community-based delinquency prevention program.
Gang	A gang is a group of individuals who share a common identity and, in current usage, engage in illegal activities. Historically the term referred to both criminal groups and ordinary groups of friends.
Control group	A group of people in an experiment who are not exposed to the experimental stimulus under study are referred to as a control group.
Statistics	Statistics is a mathematical science pertaining to the collection, analysis, interpretation, and presentation of data. It is applicable to a wide variety of academic disciplines, from the physical and social sciences to the humanities; it is also used and misused for making informed decisions in all areas of business and government.
Subculture	A group within the broader society that has values, norms and lifestyle distinct from those of the majority, is referred to as a subculture.
Norm	In sociology, a norm, or social norm, is a rule that is socially enforced. Social sanctioning is what distinguishes norms from other cultural products such as meaning and values.
Social support	Social support is the physical and emotional comfort given to us by our family, friends, co-workers and others. It is knowing that we are part of a community of people who love and care for us, and value and think well of us.
Empirical study	An empirical study in social sciences is when the research ends are based on evidence and not just theory. This is done to comply with the scientific method that asserts the objective discovery of knowledge based on verifiable facts of evidence.

Go to **Cram101.com** for the Practice Tests for this Chapter.

Go to **Cram101.com** for the Practice Tests for this Chapter.
And, **NEVER** highlight a book again!

Dispersion	The distribution of values around some central value, such as an average is referred to as a dispersion. The range is a simple example of a measure of dispersion.
White flight	White flight is a colloquial term for the demographic trend of upper and middle class Americans (predominantly white) moving away from inner cities (predominantly non-white), finding new homes in nearby suburbs or even moving to new locales entirely.
Social institution	Social institution is a group of social positions, connected by social relations, performing a social role. It can be also defined in a narrow sense as any institution in a society that works to socialize the groups or people in it.
Family disruption	Family disruption refers to the behaviors associated with altering or terminating family and pseudo-family units; separation, annulment, divorce, disownment, death, etc.
Divorce rate	The number of divorces over a specified period per specified popularion.The divorce rate is often calculated per 1,000 population or by estimating the proportion of all marriages that are expected to end in divorce.
Crime rate	Crime rate is a measure of the rate of occurrence of crimes committed in a given area and time. Most commonly, crime rate is given as the number of crimes committed among a given number of persons.
Social capital	Social capital is defined as the advantage created by a person's location in a structure of relationships. It explains how some people gain more success in a particular setting through their superior connections to other people. There are in fact a variety of inter-related definitions of this term, which has been described as "something of a cure-all" (Portes, 1998) for all the problems afflicting communities and societies today.
Coleman	Coleman was a sociological theorist, who studied the sociology of education, public policy, and was one of the earliest users of the term "social capital". His Foundations of Social Theory stands as one of the most important sociological contributions of the late-20th century.
Wilson	In The Declining Significance of Race: Blacks and Changing American Institutions Wilson argues that the significance of race is waning, and an African-American's class is comparatively more important in determining his or her life chances.
Human capital	Human capital is a way of defining and categorizing peoples' skills and abilities as used in employment and as they otherwise contribute to the economy. Many early economic theories refer to it simply as labor, one of three factors of production, and consider it to be a commodity.
Peer group	A friendship group with common interests and position composed of individuals of similar age is referred to as a peer group.
Collective efficacy	Collective efficacy is defined as a group's shared belief, which emerges from an aggregation of individual group members' perception of the group's capabilities to succeed at a given task.
Social forces	Social forces are the typical basic drives, or motives, which lead to the fundamental types of association and group relationship.
Immigration	Although human migration has existed for hundreds of thousands of years, immigration in the modern sense refers to movement of people from one nation-state to another, where they are not citizens.
Social disorganization theory	Social disorganization theory argues that delinquency is a product of the social forces existing in inner-city, low-income areas.

Go to **Cram101.com** for the Practice Tests for this Chapter.

Go to **Cram101.com** for the Practice Tests for this Chapter.
And, **NEVER** highlight a book again!

Authority	Authority refers to power that is attached to a position that others perceive as legitimate.
Census	A census is the process of obtaining information about every member of a population. It can be contrasted with sampling in which information is only obtained from a subset of a population. As such it is a method used for accumulating statistical data, and it is also vital to democracy.
Social cohesion	Social cohesion is a state in society in which the vast majority of citizens respect the law, one another's human rights and values, and share a commitment to retain social order.
Violent crime	A violent crime or crime of violence is a crime in which the offender uses or threatens to use violent force upon the victim. The United States Department of Justice Bureau of Justice Statistics (BJS) counts five categories of crime as violent crimes: murder, rape, robbery, aggravated assault, and simple assault.
Research methods	The diverse strategies used to gather empirical material in a systematic way are research methods.
Case Study	Case study refers to a research design that focuses on a single example rather than a representative sample.
Classism	Classism is any form of prejudice or oppression against people who are in, or who are perceived as being like those who are in, a lower social class (especially in the form of lower or higher socioeconomic status) within a class society.
Social interaction	Social interaction is a dynamic, changing sequence of social actions between individuals (or groups) who modify their actions and reactions due to the actions by their interaction partner(s). In other words they are events in which people attach meaning to a situation, interpret what others are meaning, and respond accordingly.
Frequency	In statistics the frequency of an event i is the number n_i of times the event occurred in the experiment or the study.
Public health	Public health is concerned with threats to the overall health of a community based on population health analysis.
Child abuse	Child abuse refers to not only physical assaults on a child but also malnourishment, abandonment, neglect, emotional abuse and sexual abuse.
Range	A measure of variability defined as the high score in a distribution minus the low score is referred to as a range.

Go to **Cram101.com** for the Practice Tests for this Chapter.

Go to **Cram101.com** for the Practice Tests for this Chapter.
And, **NEVER** highlight a book again!

Social change	Social change refers to alteration in social structures or culture over time.
Durkheim	Durkheim sought to create one of the first scientific approaches to social phenomena. Along with Herbert Spencer, Durkheim was one of the first people to explain the existence and quality of different parts of a society by reference to what function they served in keeping the society healthy and balanced—a position that would come to be known as functionalism.
Society	A society is a grouping of individuals, which is characterized by common interest and may have distinctive culture and institutions.
Merton	Merton coined the phrase "self-fulfilling prophecy." He also coined many other phrases that have gone into everyday use, such as "role model" and "unintended consequences".
Strain theory	The proposition that people feel strain when they are exposed to cultural goals that they are unable to obtain because they do not have access to culturally approved means of achieving those goals is strain theory.
Anomie	Durkheim's designation for a condition in which social control becomes ineffective as a result of the loss of shared values and a sense of purpose in society is defined as anomie.
Social Theory and Social Structure	Social Theory and Social Structure was a landmark publication in sociology by Robert K. Merton. The book introduced many important concepts in sociology, like: manifest and latent functions and dysfunctions, obliteration by incorporation, reference groups, self-fulfilling prophecy, middle-range theory and others.
Opportunity structure	The distribution of opportunities to achieve goals in a social system is referred to as an opportunity structure.
Social structure	The term social structure, used in a general sense, refers to entities or groups in definite relation to each other, to relatively enduring patterns of behavior and relationship within social systems, or to social institutions and norms becoming embedded into social systems in such a way that they shape the behavior of actors within those social systems.
Anomie Theory	Merton's theory of deviance which holds that many forms of deviance are caused by a disjunction between society's goals and the approved means to achieve these goal is referred to as anomie theory.
Social theory	Social theory refers to the use of theoretical frameworks to explain and analyze social patterns and large-scale social structures. Social theory attempts to answer the question 'what is?', not 'what should be?'. One should therefore not confuse it with philosophy or with belief.
Criminology	Criminology refers to the systematic study of crime and the criminal justice system, including the police, courts, and prisons.
Social status	Social status refers to a position in a social relationship, a characteristic that locates individuals in relation to other people and sets of role expectations.
Prestige	Prestige refers to social respect accorded to an individual or group because of the status of their position.
Ideology	Ideology refers to shared ideas or beliefs which serve to justify and support the interests of a particular group or organizations.
Norm	In sociology, a norm, or social norm, is a rule that is socially enforced. Social sanctioning is what distinguishes norms from other cultural products such as meaning and values.
Mean	In statistics, mean has two related meanings: a)the average in ordinary English, which is also called the arithmetic mean (and is distinguished from the geometric mean or harmonic mean). The average is also called sample mean. b)the expected value of a random variable, which is also called the population mean.

Go to **Cram101.com** for the Practice Tests for this Chapter.

Go to **Cram101.com** for the Practice Tests for this Chapter.
And, **NEVER** highlight a book again!

Deferred gratification	The willingness to put off the satisfaction of present desires in order for a greater gain in the future, is referred to as deferred gratification.
Crime	Crime refers to any action that violates criminal laws established by political authority. A crime in a nontechnical sense is an act that violates a very important political or moral command.
Crime rate	Crime rate is a measure of the rate of occurrence of crimes committed in a given area and time. Most commonly, crime rate is given as the number of crimes committed among a given number of persons.
Upper class	Upper class refers to a social class roughly composed of the more affluent members of society, especially those who have great wealth, control over businesses or hold large numbers of stocks and shares.
Attitude	Attitude refers to an enduring mental representation of a person, place, or thing that evokes an emotional response and related behavior.
Retreatism	A form of deviance in which a person withdraws from social life by rejecting values and norms without offering alternatives is referred to as retreatism.
Conformity	Conformity is the act of consciously maintaining a certain degree of similarity (in clothing, manners, behaviors, etc.) to those in your general social circles, to those in authority, or to the general status quo. Usually, conformity implies a tendency to submit to others in thought and behavior other than simply clothing choice.
Rebellion	A rebellion is, in the most general sense, a refusal to accept authority. It may therefore be seen as encompassing a range of behaviors from civil disobedience to a violent organized attempt to destroy established authority. It is often used in reference to armed resistance against an established government, but can also refer to mass nonviolent resistance movements.
Ritualism	Outward conformity to norms without a commitment to values they support is ritualism.
Adaptation	Adaptation refers to the ability of a sociocultural system to change with the demands of a changing physical or social environment.
Addict	A person with an overpowering physical or psychological need to continue taking a particular substance or drug is referred to as an addict.
Ritual	A ritual is a set of actions, performed mainly for their symbolic value, which is prescribed by a religion or by the traditions of a community.
Deviant behavior	Deviant behavior is behavior that is a recognized violation of social norms. Formal and informal social controls attempt to prevent and minimize deviance. One such control is through the medicalization of deviance.
Social control	A social mechanism that regulates individual and group behavior through sanctions and rewards is a social control.
Criminal law	Criminal law (also known as penal law) is the body of statutory and common law that deals with crime and the legal punishment of criminal offenses. There are four theories of criminal justice: punishment, deterrence, incapacitation, and rehabilitation.
Neighborhood	A neighborhood is a geographically localized community located within a larger city, town or suburb. Traditionally, a neighborhood is small enough that the neighbors are all able to know each other.
Gang	A gang is a group of individuals who share a common identity and, in current usage, engage in illegal activities. Historically the term referred to both criminal groups and ordinary groups of friends.

Go to **Cram101.com** for the Practice Tests for this Chapter.

Go to **Cram101.com** for the Practice Tests for this Chapter.
And, **NEVER** highlight a book again!

Achieved Status	Achieved status is a sociological term denoting a social position that a person assumes voluntarily which reflects personal skills, abilities, and efforts.
Ascribed status	Ascribed status is a social status a person is given from birth or assumes involuntarily later in life. For example, a person born into a wealthy family has a high ascribed status.
Social class	A category of people who occupy a similar position in relation to the means through which goods and services are produced in a society is a social class.
Illegitimate opportunity	Illegitimate opportunity theory holds that individuals commit crimes when the chances of being caught are low.
Organization	In sociology organization is understood as planned, coordinated and purposeful action of human beings to construct or compile a common tangible or intangible product or service.
Community	Community refers to a group of people who share a common sense of identity and interact with one another on a sustained basis.
Subculture	A group within the broader society that has values, norms and lifestyle distinct from those of the majority, is referred to as a subculture.
Juvenile delinquency	Juvenile delinquency refers to antisocial or criminal acts performed by minors. It is an important social issue because juveniles are capable of committing serious crimes, but most legal systems prescribe specific procedures and punishments for dealing with such crimes.
Delinquency prevention	That which involves any nonjustice program or policy designed to prevent the occurrence of a future delinquent act is referred to as delinquency prevention.
War on poverty	War on poverty refers to a term used to describe an overall effort of the government through federal programs to eliminate poverty in the 1960s.
Bureaucracy	Bureaucracy refers to a formal organization marked by a clear hierarchy of authority, the existence of written rules of procedure, staffed by full-time salaried officials, and striving for the efficient attainment of organizational goals.
Validity	The degree to which a measurement instrument measures what it is intended to measure is referred to as validity.
Aggregate	Aggregate refers to a collection of people who happen to be in the same place at the same time.
Punishment	Punishment is the practice of imposing something unpleasant on a subject as a response to some unwanted behavior or disobedience that the subject has displayed.
Negative relationship	A relationship in which high scores on one variable are related to low scores on another is a negative relationship.
Coping	Efforts to control, reduce, or learn to tolerate the threats that lead to stress is referred to as coping.
American Dream	The American Dream is a subjective term usually implying a successful and satisfying life. This term usually implies financial security and material comfort, but can also imply a dream of fame, exceeding social, ethnic, or class boundaries, or simply living a fulfilling life. Perceptions of the American dream are usually framed in terms of American capitalism, its associated meritocracy, and the freedoms guaranteed by the U.S. Bill of Rights.
Adolescence	Adolescence is the transitional stage of human development in which a juvenile matures into an adult. This transition involves biological (i.e. pubertal), social, and psychological changes, though the biological ones are the easiest to measure objectively.
Variable	A characteristic that varies in value or magnitude along which an object, individual or group may be categorized, such as income or age, is referred to as a variable.

Go to **Cram101.com** for the Practice Tests for this Chapter.
And, **NEVER** highlight a book again!

Social forces	Social forces are the typical basic drives, or motives, which lead to the fundamental types of association and group relationship.
Gender	Gender refers to socially defined behavior regarded as appropriate for the members of each
Criminal justice	Criminal justice refers to the system used by government to maintain social control, enforce laws, and administer justice. Law enforcement (police), courts, and corrections are the primary agencies charged with these responsibilities.
Social institution	Social institution is a group of social positions, connected by social relations, performing a social role. It can be also defined in a narrow sense as any institution in a society that works to socialize the groups or people in it.
Political institution	The relatively permanent social system through which power is distributed and exercized in societies, is referred to as a political system or political institution.
Mixed economy	A mixed economy is an economy that has a mix of economic systems. It is usually defined as an economy that contains both private-owned and state-owned enterprises or that combines elements of capitalism and socialism, or a mix of market economy and command economy.
Truly disadvantaged	According to William Julius Wilson, those people who are left out of the economic mainstream and reduced to living in the most deteriorated inner-city areas are referred to as truly disadvantaged.
Social problem	A social condition that is perceived as having harmful effects is a social problem. Opinions about whether a condition is a social problem vary among groups and depend upon how and by whom the condition is defined and perceived in society.
Welfare state	A government system which provides a range of human services for its citizens is referred to as a welfare state.
Parsons	Parsons was an advocate of "grand theory," an attempt to integrate all the social sciences into an overarching theoretical framework. His early work — The Structure of Social Action —reviewed the output of his great predecessors, especially Max Weber, Vilfredo Pareto, and Émile Durkheim, and attempted to derive from them a single "action theory" based on the assumptions that human action is voluntary, intentional, and symbolic.
Government	A government is a body that has the authority to make and the power to enforce laws within a civil, corporate, religious, academic, or other organization or group.
Public policy	Public policy is a course of action or inaction chosen by public authorities to address a problem. Public policy is expressed in the body of laws, regulations, decisions and actions of government.
Charles Murray	Charles Murray is an influential conservative American policy writer and researcher. He is most widely known for Losing Ground, his influential work on welfare reform.

Go to **Cram101.com** for the Practice Tests for this Chapter.
And, **NEVER** highlight a book again!

Merton	Merton coined the phrase "self-fulfilling prophecy." He also coined many other phrases that have gone into everyday use, such as "role model" and "unintended consequences".
Crime	Crime refers to any action that violates criminal laws established by political authority. A crime in a nontechnical sense is an act that violates a very important political or moral command.
Subculture	A group within the broader society that has values, norms and lifestyle distinct from those of the majority, is referred to as a subculture.
Gang	A gang is a group of individuals who share a common identity and, in current usage, engage in illegal activities. Historically the term referred to both criminal groups and ordinary groups of friends.
Cultural deviance theory	That which links delinquent acts to the formation of independent subcultures with a unique set of values that clash with the mainstream culture is cultural deviance theory. The cultural deviance theory would state that juvenile delinquency is a function of the enviroment.
Differential Association	In criminology, Differential Association is a theory developed by Edwin Sutherland proposing that through interaction with others, individuals learn the values, attitudes, techniques, and motives for criminal behavior.
Criminology	Criminology refers to the systematic study of crime and the criminal justice system, including the police, courts, and prisons.
Social structure	The term social structure, used in a general sense, refers to entities or groups in definite relation to each other, to relatively enduring patterns of behavior and relationship within social systems, or to social institutions and norms becoming embedded into social systems in such a way that they shape the behavior of actors within those social systems.
Deviant behavior	Deviant behavior is behavior that is a recognized violation of social norms. Formal and informal social controls attempt to prevent and minimize deviance. One such control is through the medicalization of deviance.
Social learning	The process through which we acquire new information, forms of behavior, or attitudes exclusively or primarily in a social group, is referred to as a social learning.
Punishment	Punishment is the practice of imposing something unpleasant on a subject as a response to some unwanted behavior or disobedience that the subject has displayed.
Social learning theory	A theory emphasizing that boys develop maleness and girls develop femaleness through exposure to scores of influence-including parents, peers, television, and schools-that teach them what it means to be a man or a woman in their culture, is referred to as a social learning theory.
Bandura	Bandura is most famous for his work on social learning theory (or Social Cognitivism) and self efficacy.
Tarde	Tarde conceived sociology as based on small psychological interactions among individuals (much as if it were chemistry), the fundamental forces being imitation and innovation.
Social class	A category of people who occupy a similar position in relation to the means through which goods and services are produced in a society is a social class.
Murder	Murder is the unlawful, premeditated killing of a human being by another. The penalty for murder is usually either life imprisonment, or in jurisdictions with capital punishment, the death penalty.
Edwin Sutherland	Edwin Sutherland (1893–1950) is considered to be one of the most influential criminologists of the twentieth century. He is best known for defining differential association which is a general theory of crime and delinquency that explains how deviants come to learn the

Go to **Cram101.com** for the Practice Tests for this Chapter.
And, **NEVER** highlight a book again!

motivations and the technical knowledge for deviant or criminal activity.

Rationalization	Rationalization is the process whereby an increasing number of social actions and interactions become based on considerations of efficiency or calculation rather than on motivations derived from custom, tradition, or emotion.
Attitude	Attitude refers to an enduring mental representation of a person, place, or thing that evokes an emotional response and related behavior.
Motive	Motive refers to a hypothetical state within an organism that propels the organism toward a goal. In criminal law a motive is the cause that moves people and induce a certain action.
Society	A society is a grouping of individuals, which is characterized by common interest and may have distinctive culture and institutions.
Frequency	In statistics the frequency of an event i is the number n_i of times the event occurred in the experiment or the study.
Social status	Social status refers to a position in a social relationship, a characteristic that locates individuals in relation to other people and sets of role expectations.
Symbolic interactionism	Symbolic interactionism refers to a theoretical approach in sociology which focuses on social reality as constructed through the daily interaction of individuals and places strong emphasis on the role of symbols as core elements of this interaction.
George Herbert Mead	George Herbert Mead is an important figure in 20th century social philosophy. His theory of how the mind and self emerge from the social process of communication by signs founded the symbolic interactionist school of sociology and social psychology.
Interactionism	Interactionism is a generic sociological perspective that brings under its umbrella a number of subperspectives: phenomenology, ethnomethodology, Symbolic interactionism (social psychology), and Social constructionism.
Embezzlement	Embezzlement is the fraudulent appropriation by a person to his own use of property or money entrusted to that person's care but owned by someone else.
Shoplifting	Shoplifting (also known as retail theft) is theft of merchandise for sale in a shop, store, or other retail establishment, by an ostensible patron. It is one of the most common crimes for police and courts.
Culture conflict	When the values of a subculture clash with those of the dominant culture, there is a culture conflict.
Social disorganization	Social disorganization refers to a structural condition of society caused by rapid change in social institutions, norms, and values.
Chicago school	In sociology and, later, criminology, the Chicago School (sometimes described as the Ecological School) refers to the first major body of works emerging during the 1920s and 1930s specializing in urban sociology, and the research into the urban environment by combining theory and ethnographic fieldwork in Chicago, now applied elsewhere.
Human ecology	Human ecology is an academic discipline that deals with the relationship between humans and their natural, social and created environments. Human ecology investigates how humans and human societies interact with nature and with their environment.
Organization	In sociology organization is understood as planned, coordinated and purposeful action of human beings to construct or compile a common tangible or intangible product or service.
Social group	A group that consists of two or more people who interact frequently and share a common identity and a feeling of interdependence, is referred to as a social group.
Norm	In sociology, a norm, or social norm, is a rule that is socially enforced. Social sanctioning

Go to **Cram101.com** for the Practice Tests for this Chapter.
And, **NEVER** highlight a book again!

is what distinguishes norms from other cultural products such as meaning and values.

Juvenile delinquency	Juvenile delinquency refers to antisocial or criminal acts performed by minors. It is an important social issue because juveniles are capable of committing serious crimes, but most legal systems prescribe specific procedures and punishments for dealing with such crimes.
Donald Cressey	Donald Cressey (1919-1987), was a penologist, sociologist and a criminologist, who is known for his studies in organized crime. Based on research conducted in this capacity he wrote the acclaimed "Theft of the Nation", a treatise on Cosa Nostra, and later a smaller volume entitled "Criminal Organization".
Epidemiology	Epidemiology is the scientific study of factors affecting the health and illness of populations, and serves as the foundation and logic of interventions made in the interest of public health and preventive medicine.
Subcultural theory	In criminology, Subcultural Theory emerged from the work of the Chicago School on gangs and developed through the Symbolic Interactionism School into a set of theories arguing that certain groups or subcultures in society have values and attitudes that are conducive to crime and violence.
Social problem	A social condition that is perceived as having harmful effects is a social problem. Opinions about whether a condition is a social problem vary among groups and depend upon how and by whom the condition is defined and perceived in society.
Control theory	A theory that views crime as the outcome of an imbalance between impulses toward criminal activity and controls that deter it is referred to as control theory. Control theorists hold that criminals are rational beings who will act to maximize their own reward.
Social forces	Social forces are the typical basic drives, or motives, which lead to the fundamental types of association and group relationship.
Gender	Gender refers to socially defined behavior regarded as appropriate for the members of each
Middle class	A social class broadly defined occupationally as those working in white-collar and lower managerial occupations and is sometimes defined by reference to income levels or subjective identification of the participants in the study are referred to as middle class.
Focal concerns	The value orientations of lower-class subculture that is characterized by a need for excitement, trouble, smartness, toughness, fate, and personal autonomy are referred to as focal concerns.
Masculinity	Masculinity refers to the characteristic forms of behavior expected of men in any given culture.
Authority	Authority refers to power that is attached to a position that others perceive as legitimate.
Autonomy	Autonomy is a concept found in moral, political, and bioethical philosophy. Within these contexts it refers to the capacity of a rational individual to make an informed, uncoerced decision. In moral and political philosophy, autonomy is often used as the basis for determining moral responsibility for one's actions.
Mean	In statistics, mean has two related meanings: a)the average in ordinary English, which is also called the arithmetic mean (and is distinguished from the geometric mean or harmonic mean). The average is also called sample mean. b)the expected value of a random variable, which is also called the population mean.
Strain theory	The proposition that people feel strain when they are exposed to cultural goals that they are unable to obtain because they do not have access to culturally approved means of achieving those goals is strain theory.
Social issue	Social issue refers to matters that can be explained only by factors outside an individual's

Go to **Cram101.com** for the Practice Tests for this Chapter.

Go to **Cram101.com** for the Practice Tests for this Chapter.
And, **NEVER** highlight a book again!

control and immediate social environment. They usually concern more than a single individual and affect many individuals in a society.

Social interaction	Social interaction is a dynamic, changing sequence of social actions between individuals (or groups) who modify their actions and reactions due to the actions by their interaction partner(s). In other words they are events in which people attach meaning to a situation, interpret what others are meaning, and respond accordingly.
Violent crime	A violent crime or crime of violence is a crime in which the offender uses or threatens to use violent force upon the victim. The United States Department of Justice Bureau of Justice Statistics (BJS) counts five categories of crime as violent crimes: murder, rape, robbery, aggravated assault, and simple assault.
Exploitation	In political economy, economics, and sociology, exploitation involves a persistent social relationship in which certain persons are being mistreated or unfairly used for the benefit of others. This corresponds to one ethical conception of exploitation, that is, the treatment of human beings as mere means to an end — or as mere "objects".
Slavery	Slavery refers to an extreme form of stratification in which some people are owned by others.
Inner city	The areas composing the central neighborhoods of industrial cities which are subject to dilapidation and decay, with the more affluent residents having moved to outlying area is an inner city.
Social research	Social research refers to research conducted by social scientists (primarily within sociology and social psychology, but also within other disciplines such as social policy, human geography, political science, social anthropology and education).
Social ecology	The entire network of interactions and interdependencies among people, institutions, and cultural constructs to which the developing person must adapt psychologically is a social ecology.
Criminal justice	Criminal justice refers to the system used by government to maintain social control, enforce laws, and administer justice. Law enforcement (police), courts, and corrections are the primary agencies charged with these responsibilities.
Peer group	A friendship group with common interests and position composed of individuals of similar age is referred to as a peer group.
Alienation	In sociology and critical social theory, alienation refers to the individual's estrangement from traditional community and others in general.
Endemic	In epidemiology, an infection is said to be endemic in a population when that infection is maintained in the population without the need for external inputs.
Racism	Racism is a belief in the moral or biological superiority of one race or ethnic group over another or others.
Truly disadvantaged	According to William Julius Wilson, those people who are left out of the economic mainstream and reduced to living in the most deteriorated inner-city areas are referred to as truly disadvantaged.
Reinforcement	A stimulus that follows a response and increases the frequency of the response is a reinforcement.
Criminal law	Criminal law (also known as penal law) is the body of statutory and common law that deals with crime and the legal punishment of criminal offenses. There are four theories of criminal justice: punishment, deterrence, incapacitation, and rehabilitation.
Glaser	Glaser, American sociologist and one of the founders of the grounded theory methodology. In 1999 Glaser founded the non-profit web based organization Grounded Theory Institute.

Go to **Cram101.com** for the Practice Tests for this Chapter.
And, **NEVER** highlight a book again!

Reference group	Individuals almost universally have a bond toward a Reference Group. These are groups to which the individual does not have real membership, but to which he conceptually relates him/herself, and from which he might accept goals and values as a part of his/her self identity.
Robbery	The unlawful taking of, or the attempt to take something of value from another person or persons by using violence or the threat of violence, is referred to as a robbery.
Criminologist	A criminologist is often defined as someone who studies the aetiology of crime, criminal behavior, types of crime, and social, cultural and media reactions to crime.
Minority group	A minority group or subordinate group is a sociological group that does not constitute a politically dominant plurality of the total population of a given society.
Crime rate	Crime rate is a measure of the rate of occurrence of crimes committed in a given area and time. Most commonly, crime rate is given as the number of crimes committed among a given number of persons.
Variable	A characteristic that varies in value or magnitude along which an object, individual or group may be categorized, such as income or age, is referred to as a variable.

Go to **Cram101.com** for the Practice Tests for this Chapter.
And, **NEVER** highlight a book again!

Crime	Crime refers to any action that violates criminal laws established by political authority. A crime in a nontechnical sense is an act that violates a very important political or moral command.
Control theory	A theory that views crime as the outcome of an imbalance between impulses toward criminal activity and controls that deter it is referred to as control theory. Control theorists hold that criminals are rational beings who will act to maximize their own reward.
Psychotherapy	Psychotherapy refers to a systematic interaction between a therapist and a client that brings psychological principles to bear on influencing the client's thoughts, feelings, or behavior to help that client overcome abnormal behavior or adjust to problems in living.
Criminology	Criminology refers to the systematic study of crime and the criminal justice system, including the police, courts, and prisons.
Community	Community refers to a group of people who share a common sense of identity and interact with one another on a sustained basis.
Probation	Nonpunitive, legal disposition of juveniles emphasizing community treatment in which the juvenile is closely supervized by an officer of the court and must adhere to a strict set of rules to avoid incarceration is probation.
Norm	In sociology, a norm, or social norm, is a rule that is socially enforced. Social sanctioning is what distinguishes norms from other cultural products such as meaning and values.
Authority	Authority refers to power that is attached to a position that others perceive as legitimate.
Social control	A social mechanism that regulates individual and group behavior through sanctions and rewards is a social control.
Conformity	Conformity is the act of consciously maintaining a certain degree of similarity (in clothing, manners, behaviors, etc.) to those in your general social circles, to those in authority, or to the general status quo. Usually, conformity implies a tendency to submit to others in thought and behavior other than simply clothing choice.
Commitment to conformity	Commitment to conformity refers to the strength of the ties of youths to conventional social institutions predicts their likely behavior; those with poor or negative ties are more likely to indulge in delinquent acts.
Social disorganization	Social disorganization refers to a structural condition of society caused by rapid change in social institutions, norms, and values.
Social problem	A social condition that is perceived as having harmful effects is a social problem. Opinions about whether a condition is a social problem vary among groups and depend upon how and by whom the condition is defined and perceived in society.
Criminal law	Criminal law (also known as penal law) is the body of statutory and common law that deals with crime and the legal punishment of criminal offenses. There are four theories of criminal justice: punishment, deterrence, incapacitation, and rehabilitation.
Crime rate	Crime rate is a measure of the rate of occurrence of crimes committed in a given area and time. Most commonly, crime rate is given as the number of crimes committed among a given number of persons.
Punishment	Punishment is the practice of imposing something unpleasant on a subject as a response to some unwanted behavior or disobedience that the subject has displayed.
Mean	In statistics, mean has two related meanings: a)the average in ordinary English, which is also called the arithmetic mean (and is distinguished from the geometric mean or harmonic mean). The average is also called sample mean. b)the expected value of a random variable, which is also called the population mean.

71

Criminologist	A criminologist is often defined as someone who studies the aetiology of crime, criminal behavior, types of crime, and social, cultural and media reactions to crime.
Juvenile delinquency	Juvenile delinquency refers to antisocial or criminal acts performed by minors. It is an important social issue because juveniles are capable of committing serious crimes, but most legal systems prescribe specific procedures and punishments for dealing with such crimes.
Compulsion	An apparently irresistible urge to repeat an act or engage in ritualistic behavior, often despite negative consequences is referred to as a compulsion.
Late adolescence	Late adolescence refers to approximately the latter half of the second decade of life. Career interests, dating, and identity exploration are often more pronounced in late adolescence than in early adolescence.
Adolescence	Adolescence is the transitional stage of human development in which a juvenile matures into an adult. This transition involves biological (i.e. pubertal), social, and psychological changes, though the biological ones are the easiest to measure objectively.
Social structure	The term social structure, used in a general sense, refers to entities or groups in definite relation to each other, to relatively enduring patterns of behavior and relationship within social systems, or to social institutions and norms becoming embedded into social systems in such a way that they shape the behavior of actors within those social systems.
Frame of reference	One's unique patterning of perceptions and attitudes according to which one evaluates and reacts to events is a frame of reference.
Insanity	Insanity refers to a legal status indicating that a person cannot be held responsible for his or her actions because of mental illness.
Social Control Theory	In criminology, Social Control Theory as represented in the work of Travis Hirschi fits into the Positivist School, Neo-Classical School, and, later, Right Realism. It proposes that exploiting the process of socialization and social learning builds self-control and reduces the inclination to indulge in behavior recognized as antisocial.
Social group	A group that consists of two or more people who interact frequently and share a common identity and a feeling of interdependence, is referred to as a social group.
Social bond	Social bond refers to ties a person to the institutions and processes of society; elements of the bond include attachment, commitment, involvement, and belief.
Deviant behavior	Deviant behavior is behavior that is a recognized violation of social norms. Formal and informal social controls attempt to prevent and minimize deviance. One such control is through the medicalization of deviance.
Society	A society is a grouping of individuals, which is characterized by common interest and may have distinctive culture and institutions.
Social class	A category of people who occupy a similar position in relation to the means through which goods and services are produced in a society is a social class.
Strain theory	The proposition that people feel strain when they are exposed to cultural goals that they are unable to obtain because they do not have access to culturally approved means of achieving those goals is strain theory.
Aptitude Test	Aptitude test refers to a test designed to predict a person's ability in a particular area or line of work.
Middle class	A social class broadly defined occupationally as those working in white-collar and lower managerial occupations and is sometimes defined by reference to income levels or subjective identification of the participants in the study are referred to as middle class.

Go to **Cram101.com** for the Practice Tests for this Chapter.

Go to **Cram101.com** for the Practice Tests for this Chapter.
And, **NEVER** highlight a book again!

Empirical study	An empirical study in social sciences is when the research ends are based on evidence and not just theory. This is done to comply with the scientific method that asserts the objective discovery of knowledge based on verifiable facts of evidence.
Variable	A characteristic that varies in value or magnitude along which an object, individual or group may be categorized, such as income or age, is referred to as a variable.
Differential Association	In criminology, Differential Association is a theory developed by Edwin Sutherland proposing that through interaction with others, individuals learn the values, attitudes, techniques, and motives for criminal behavior.
Gang	A gang is a group of individuals who share a common identity and, in current usage, engage in illegal activities. Historically the term referred to both criminal groups and ordinary groups of friends.
Violent crime	A violent crime or crime of violence is a crime in which the offender uses or threatens to use violent force upon the victim. The United States Department of Justice Bureau of Justice Statistics (BJS) counts five categories of crime as violent crimes: murder, rape, robbery, aggravated assault, and simple assault.
Control variable	A variable introduced into a statistical analysis to see if a statistical relationship holds among people who are alike on a particular characteristic is referred to as a control variable.
Social environment	The social environment is the direct influence of a group of individuals and their contributions to this environment, as both groups and individuals who are in frequent communication with each other within their cultural or socio-economical strata, which create role identity(-ies) and guide the individual's self (sociology) growth and their progression towards maturity.
Socialization	Socialization refers to the lifelong processes through which humans develop an awareness of social norms and values, and achieve a distinct sense of self.
Attitude	Attitude refers to an enduring mental representation of a person, place, or thing that evokes an emotional response and related behavior.
Subcultural theory	In criminology, Subcultural Theory emerged from the work of the Chicago School on gangs and developed through the Symbolic Interactionism School into a set of theories arguing that certain groups or subcultures in society have values and attitudes that are conducive to crime and violence.
Neoclassical criminology	The doctrinal and procedural compromise between classicism and positivism, devized roughly between 1890 and 1910, that has become the basis of criminal responsibility and punishment in most Western societies with its emphasis on free will and individual choice as the root causes of crime, is referred to as neoclassical criminology.
Criminal justice	Criminal justice refers to the system used by government to maintain social control, enforce laws, and administer justice. Law enforcement (police), courts, and corrections are the primary agencies charged with these responsibilities.
Range	A measure of variability defined as the high score in a distribution minus the low score is referred to as a range.
Validity	The degree to which a measurement instrument measures what it is intended to measure is referred to as validity.

Go to **Cram101.com** for the Practice Tests for this Chapter.

Go to **Cram101.com** for the Practice Tests for this Chapter.
And, **NEVER** highlight a book again!

Crime	Crime refers to any action that violates criminal laws established by political authority. A crime in a nontechnical sense is an act that violates a very important political or moral command.
Criminal justice	Criminal justice refers to the system used by government to maintain social control, enforce laws, and administer justice. Law enforcement (police), courts, and corrections are the primary agencies charged with these responsibilities.
Criminologist	A criminologist is often defined as someone who studies the aetiology of crime, criminal behavior, types of crime, and social, cultural and media reactions to crime.
Criminology	Criminology refers to the systematic study of crime and the criminal justice system, including the police, courts, and prisons.
Positivism	A philosophical position according to which there are close ties between the social and natural sciences, which share a common logical framework is positivism.
Deterrence	Deterrence is a theory from behavioral psychology about preventing or controlling actions or behavior through fear of punishment or retribution. This theory of criminology is shaping the criminal justice system of the United States and various other countries.
Punishment	Punishment is the practice of imposing something unpleasant on a subject as a response to some unwanted behavior or disobedience that the subject has displayed.
Mean	In statistics, mean has two related meanings: a)the average in ordinary English, which is also called the arithmetic mean (and is distinguished from the geometric mean or harmonic mean). The average is also called sample mean. b)the expected value of a random variable, which is also called the population mean.
Social problem	A social condition that is perceived as having harmful effects is a social problem. Opinions about whether a condition is a social problem vary among groups and depend upon how and by whom the condition is defined and perceived in society.
Social forces	Social forces are the typical basic drives, or motives, which lead to the fundamental types of association and group relationship.
Jurisdiction	Jurisdiction refers to every kind of judicial action; the authority of courts and judicial officers to decide cases.
Crime rate	Crime rate is a measure of the rate of occurrence of crimes committed in a given area and time. Most commonly, crime rate is given as the number of crimes committed among a given number of persons.
Sanction	A punishment for nonconformity that reinforces socially approved forms of behavior is a sanction.
Murder	Murder is the unlawful, premeditated killing of a human being by another. The penalty for murder is usually either life imprisonment, or in jurisdictions with capital punishment, the death penalty.
Glaser	Glaser, American sociologist and one of the founders of the grounded theory methodology. In 1999 Glaser founded the non-profit web based organization Grounded Theory Institute.
Empirical research	Empirical research is any research that bases its findings on direct or indirect observation as its test of reality. Such research may also be conducted according to hypothetico-deductive procedures, such as those developed from the work of R. A. Fisher.
Consensus	Agreement on basic social values by the members of a group or society is referred to as a consensus.
Public policy	Public policy is a course of action or inaction chosen by public authorities to address a

Go to **Cram101.com** for the Practice Tests for this Chapter.
And, **NEVER** highlight a book again!

	problem. Public policy is expressed in the body of laws, regulations, decisions and actions of government.
Violent crime	A violent crime or crime of violence is a crime in which the offender uses or threatens to use violent force upon the victim. The United States Department of Justice Bureau of Justice Statistics (BJS) counts five categories of crime as violent crimes: murder, rape, robbery, aggravated assault, and simple assault.
Statistics	Statistics is a mathematical science pertaining to the collection, analysis, interpretation, and presentation of data. It is applicable to a wide variety of academic disciplines, from the physical and social sciences to the humanities; it is also used and misused for making informed decisions in all areas of business and government.
Capital punishment	Use of the death penalty to punish offenders is called capital punishment.
Criminal law	Criminal law (also known as penal law) is the body of statutory and common law that deals with crime and the legal punishment of criminal offenses. There are four theories of criminal justice: punishment, deterrence, incapacitation, and rehabilitation.
Society	A society is a grouping of individuals, which is characterized by common interest and may have distinctive culture and institutions.
Sector	Sector refers to parts of the economy as judged by the economic activity that they constitute. For example agriculture, forestry, fishing and mining constitute the primary sector.
Three strikes law	The three strikes law is a highly controversial category of statutes enacted by state governments in the United States which require the state courts to hand down a mandatory and extended period of incarceration to persons who have been convicted of a serious criminal offense on three or more separate occasions.
Felony	The term felony is used for very serious crimes, whereas misdemeanors are considered to be less serious offenses. It is a crime punishable by one or more years of imprisonment.
Rational choice	Rational choice theory assumes human behavior is guided by instrumental reason. Accordingly, individuals always choose what they believe to be the best means to achieve their given ends. Thus, they are normally regarded as maximizing utility, the "currency" for everything they cherish (for example: money, a long life, moral standards).
Social institution	Social institution is a group of social positions, connected by social relations, performing a social role. It can be also defined in a narrow sense as any institution in a society that works to socialize the groups or people in it.
Choice theory	Choice Theory posits that behavior is central to our existence and is driven by five genetically driven needs, similar to those of Maslow: 1)Survival and four fundamental psychological needs: 2)Belonging/connecting/love, 3)Power, 4)Freedom, and 5)Fun.
Situational crime prevention	A crime prevention method that relies on reducing the opportunity to commit criminal acts by making them more difficult to perform, reducing their reward and increasing their risks is situational crime prevention.
Crime prevention	Crime prevention is a term describing techniques used in reducing victimization as well as deterring crime and criminals. It is applied specifically to efforts made by governments to reduce crime and law enforcement and criminal justice.
Case Study	Case study refers to a research design that focuses on a single example rather than a representative sample.
Range	A measure of variability defined as the high score in a distribution minus the low score is

Go to **Cram101.com** for the Practice Tests for this Chapter.
And, **NEVER** highlight a book again!

referred to as a range.

Predatory crime	A violent crime with a human victim or a crime in which an offender attempts to steal an object directly from its holder is a predatory crime.
Social change	Social change refers to alteration in social structures or culture over time.
Social indicators	Social indicators refers to measurements that reflect the quality or nature of social life, such as crime rates, infant mortality rates, number of physicians per 100,000 population, and so forth.
Organization	In sociology organization is understood as planned, coordinated and purposeful action of human beings to construct or compile a common tangible or intangible product or service.
Routine activities theory	Routine activities theory claims that patterns of crime and victimization are the result of the everyday interaction of likely offenders, suitable targets, and guardians.
Durkheim	Durkheim sought to create one of the first scientific approaches to social phenomena. Along with Herbert Spencer, Durkheim was one of the first people to explain the existence and quality of different parts of a society by reference to what function they served in keeping the society healthy and balanced—a position that would come to be known as functionalism.
Berger	Berger is perhaps best known for his view that social reality is a form of consciousness. Central to his work is the relationship between society and the individual. In his book The Social Construction of Reality Berger develops a sociological theory: 'Society as Objective Reality and as Subjective Reality'. His analysis of society as subjective reality describes the process by which an individual's conception of reality is produced by his or her interaction with social structures.
Community	Community refers to a group of people who share a common sense of identity and interact with one another on a sustained basis.
Validity	The degree to which a measurement instrument measures what it is intended to measure is referred to as validity.

Go to **Cram101.com** for the Practice Tests for this Chapter.
And, **NEVER** highlight a book again!

Classical criminology	Criminology based on both free will and determinism and whose chief aim was to deter crime refers to classical criminology. It was part of the humanist reaction during the Enlightenment to the barbarities and inequities characteristic of feudal systems of justice.
Criminology	Criminology refers to the systematic study of crime and the criminal justice system, including the police, courts, and prisons.
Symbolic interactionism	Symbolic interactionism refers to a theoretical approach in sociology which focuses on social reality as constructed through the daily interaction of individuals and places strong emphasis on the role of symbols as core elements of this interaction.
Interactionism	Interactionism is a generic sociological perspective that brings under its umbrella a number of subperspectives: phenomenology, ethnomethodology, Symbolic interactionism (social psychology), and Social constructionism.
Labeling theory	A social theory that holds that society's reaction to certain behaviors is a major factor in defining the self as deviant is labeling theory.
Labeling	Labeling is defining or describing a person in terms of his or her behavior. The term is often used in sociology to describe human interaction, control and identification of deviant behavior.
Criminologist	A criminologist is often defined as someone who studies the aetiology of crime, criminal behavior, types of crime, and social, cultural and media reactions to crime.
Crime	Crime refers to any action that violates criminal laws established by political authority. A crime in a nontechnical sense is an act that violates a very important political or moral command.
Society	A society is a grouping of individuals, which is characterized by common interest and may have distinctive culture and institutions.
Symbolic interaction theory	Symbolic interaction theory refers to a theory that describes the family as a unit of interacting personalities communicating through symbols.
Symbolic interaction	Symbolic interaction refers to the use of symbols by people to present themselves to others and interpret one another's behavior.
Social interaction	Social interaction is a dynamic, changing sequence of social actions between individuals (or groups) who modify their actions and reactions due to the actions by their interaction partner(s). In other words they are events in which people attach meaning to a situation, interpret what others are meaning, and respond accordingly.
Cooley	Cooley was an American sociologist whose concept of the "looking glass self" is undoubtedly his most famous, and is known and accepted by most psychologists and sociologists today. It expanded William James's idea of self to include the capacity of reflection on its own behavior. Other people's views build, change and maintain our self-image; thus, there is an interaction between how we see ourselves and how others see us.
Social psychology	Social psychology refers to the study of the effects of social environments on the psychological functioning of individuals.
Social order	Social order refers to a set of linked social structures, social institutions and social practices which conserve, maintain and enforce "normal" ways of relating and behaving.
Neighborhood	A neighborhood is a geographically localized community located within a larger city, town or suburb. Traditionally, a neighborhood is small enough that the neighbors are all able to know each other.
Deviant behavior	Deviant behavior is behavior that is a recognized violation of social norms. Formal and

Go to **Cram101.com** for the Practice Tests for this Chapter.
And, **NEVER** highlight a book again!

	informal social controls attempt to prevent and minimize deviance. One such control is through the medicalization of deviance.
Social problem	A social condition that is perceived as having harmful effects is a social problem. Opinions about whether a condition is a social problem vary among groups and depend upon how and by whom the condition is defined and perceived in society.
Social control	A social mechanism that regulates individual and group behavior through sanctions and rewards is a social control.
Community	Community refers to a group of people who share a common sense of identity and interact with one another on a sustained basis.
Embezzlement	Embezzlement is the fraudulent appropriation by a person to his own use of property or money entrusted to that person's care but owned by someone else.
Techniques of neutralization	Techniques of neutralization are a series of methods by which, it is believed, those who commit illegitimate acts temporarily neutralize certain values within themselves which would normally prohibit them from carrying out such acts, such as morality, obligation to abide by the law, and so on.
Degradation ceremony	An important part of the socialization process in total institutions, in which inmates are subjected to humiliation and labeled as inferior is a degradation ceremony.
Garfinkel	Garfinkel is one of the key developers of the phenomenological tradition in American sociology. His own development of this tradition (which he terms ethnomethodology) is widely misunderstood. In contrast to the social constructionist version of phenomenological sociology, he emphasises a focus on radical phenomena, rather than on the various ways they are interpreted.
Sociology of deviance	The sociology of deviance is the sociological study of deviant behavior, the recognized violation of cultural norms, and the creation and enforcement of those norms.
Stereotype	A stereotype refers to widely shared beliefs about the characteristic traits, attitudes, and behaviors of members of various social groups, including the assumption that the members of such groups are usually all alike.
Heroin	A highly addictive, partly synthetic narcotic derived from morphine is heroin. It mimics endorphins and thus causes a high sense of well-being when entered into the bloodstream (usually through injection).
Addict	A person with an overpowering physical or psychological need to continue taking a particular substance or drug is referred to as an addict.
Social forces	Social forces are the typical basic drives, or motives, which lead to the fundamental types of association and group relationship.
Deterrence	Deterrence is a theory from behavioral psychology about preventing or controlling actions or behavior through fear of punishment or retribution. This theory of criminology is shaping the criminal justice system of the United States and various other countries.
Punishment	Punishment is the practice of imposing something unpleasant on a subject as a response to some unwanted behavior or disobedience that the subject has displayed.
Gender	Gender refers to socially defined behavior regarded as appropriate for the members of each
Variable	A characteristic that varies in value or magnitude along which an object, individual or group may be categorized, such as income or age, is referred to as a variable.
Participant observation	Participant observation is a major research strategy which aims to gain a close and intimate familiarity with a given group of individuals (such as a religious, occupational, or deviant

Go to Cram101.com for the Practice Tests for this Chapter.

Go to **Cram101.com** for the Practice Tests for this Chapter.
And, **NEVER** highlight a book again!

group) and their practices through an intensive involvement with people in their natural environment.

Shoplifting	Shoplifting (also known as retail theft) is theft of merchandise for sale in a shop, store, or other retail establishment, by an ostensible patron. It is one of the most common crimes for police and courts.
Gang	A gang is a group of individuals who share a common identity and, in current usage, engage in illegal activities. Historically the term referred to both criminal groups and ordinary groups of friends.
Robbery	The unlawful taking of, or the attempt to take something of value from another person or persons by using violence or the threat of violence, is referred to as a robbery.
Dominance	In animal colonies, a condition established by one animal over another by prevailing in an aggressive encounter between the two, is referred to as dominance.
Ethnography	A detailed study of the life and activities of a group of people by researchers who may live with that group over a period of years, is referred to as an ethnography.
Wright	Wright is an American sociologist. His work is concerned mainly with the study of social classes, and in particular with the task of providing an update to the Marxist concept of class. Wright has stressed the importance of the control of the means of production in defining 'class', while at the same trying to account for the situation of skilled employees, taking inspiration from Weberian accounts of authority.
Criminal justice	Criminal justice refers to the system used by government to maintain social control, enforce laws, and administer justice. Law enforcement (police), courts, and corrections are the primary agencies charged with these responsibilities.
Solidarity	Solidarity in sociology refers to the feeling or condition of unity based on common goals, interests, and sympathies among a group's members. Solidarity refers to the ties in a society - social relations - that bind people to one another.
Verstehen	Verstehen was used by Max Weber to describe a process in which outside observers of a culture relate to an indigenous people on their own terms, rather than interpreting them in terms of the observers own concepts.
Criminalization	Criminalization refers to the process whereby criminal law is selectively applied to social behavior. It involves the enactment of legislation that outlaws certain types of behavior and provides for surveillance and policing of that behavior and whether or not the behavior is detected.
Acquisition	The initial learning of the stimulus response link, which involves a neutral stimulus being associated with a UCS and becoming a conditioned stimulus, is referred to as an acquisition.
Alcoholism	Alcoholism refers to a disorder that involves long-term, repeated, uncontrolled, compulsive, and excessive use of alcoholic beverages and that impairs the drinker's health, work and social relationships.
Addiction	A pattern of behavior characterized by an overwhelming involvement with using a drug and securing its supply is defined as an addiction.
Narcotic	A narcotic is an addictive drug, derived from opium, that reduces pain, induces sleep and may alter mood or behavior.
Bureaucracy	Bureaucracy refers to a formal organization marked by a clear hierarchy of authority, the existence of written rules of procedure, staffed by full-time salaried officials, and striving for the efficient attainment of organizational goals.
Identity	Identity politics is the political activity of various social movements for self-

Go to **Cram101.com** for the Practice Tests for this Chapter.
And, **NEVER** highlight a book again!

politics	determination. It claims to represent and seek to advance the interests of particular groups in society.
Organized crime	Organized crime is crime carried out systematically by formal criminal organizations.
Criminal law	Criminal law (also known as penal law) is the body of statutory and common law that deals with crime and the legal punishment of criminal offenses. There are four theories of criminal justice: punishment, deterrence, incapacitation, and rehabilitation.
Hate crime	A hate crime (also known as bias crime) is a violent crime, hate speech or vandalism, motivated by feelings of enmity against an identifiable social group.
Sanction	A punishment for nonconformity that reinforces socially approved forms of behavior is a sanction.
Foucault	Foucault is known for his critical studies of various social institutions, most notably psychiatry, medicine, parameters of educational timeframes, and the prison system, and also for his work on the history of sexuality.
Torture	Torture is the infliction of pain intended to break the will of the victim or victims. Any act by which severe pain, whether physical or psychological, is intentionally inflicted on a person as a means of intimidation, deterrence, revenge, punishment, sadism, or to obtain confessions (true or false) for propaganda or political purposes may be called torture.
Insanity	Insanity refers to a legal status indicating that a person cannot be held responsible for his or her actions because of mental illness.
Range	A measure of variability defined as the high score in a distribution minus the low score is referred to as a range.
Norm	In sociology, a norm, or social norm, is a rule that is socially enforced. Social sanctioning is what distinguishes norms from other cultural products such as meaning and values.

Go to **Cram101.com** for the Practice Tests for this Chapter.

Go to **Cram101.com** for the Practice Tests for this Chapter.
And, **NEVER** highlight a book again!

Consensus	Agreement on basic social values by the members of a group or society is referred to as a consensus.
Society	A society is a grouping of individuals, which is characterized by common interest and may have distinctive culture and institutions.
Social theory	Social theory refers to the use of theoretical frameworks to explain and analyze social patterns and large-scale social structures. Social theory attempts to answer the question 'what is?', not 'what should be?'. One should therefore not confuse it with philosophy or with belief.
Criminology	Criminology refers to the systematic study of crime and the criminal justice system, including the police, courts, and prisons.
Crime rate	Crime rate is a measure of the rate of occurrence of crimes committed in a given area and time. Most commonly, crime rate is given as the number of crimes committed among a given number of persons.
Crime	Crime refers to any action that violates criminal laws established by political authority. A crime in a nontechnical sense is an act that violates a very important political or moral command.
Conflict theory	Conflict theory or conflict perspective refers to a theory that conflict is normal and that the task is not to eliminate conflict but to learn to control it so that it becomes constructive.
Conduct norm	A rule of behavior that embodies the values of a particular group in society is a conduct norm.
Norm	In sociology, a norm, or social norm, is a rule that is socially enforced. Social sanctioning is what distinguishes norms from other cultural products such as meaning and values.
Migration	The movement of people from one country or region to another in order to settle permanently, is referred to as a migration.
Subculture	A group within the broader society that has values, norms and lifestyle distinct from those of the majority, is referred to as a subculture.
Culture conflict	When the values of a subculture clash with those of the dominant culture, there is a culture conflict.
Social order	Social order refers to a set of linked social structures, social institutions and social practices which conserve, maintain and enforce "normal" ways of relating and behaving.
Collective action	Collective action is the pursuit of a goal or set of goals by more than one person.
Criminal justice	Criminal justice refers to the system used by government to maintain social control, enforce laws, and administer justice. Law enforcement (police), courts, and corrections are the primary agencies charged with these responsibilities.
Civil Rights Movement	Historically, the civil rights movement was a concentrated period of time around the world of approximately one generation (1954-1980) wherein there was much worldwide civil unrest and popular rebellion.
Civil rights	Civil rights are the protections and privileges of personal liberty given to all citizens by law. Civil rights are rights that are bestowed by nations on those within their territorial boundaries.
Criminal law	Criminal law (also known as penal law) is the body of statutory and common law that deals with crime and the legal punishment of criminal offenses. There are four theories of criminal

Go to Cram101.com for the Practice Tests for this Chapter.

Go to **Cram101.com** for the Practice Tests for this Chapter.
And, **NEVER** highlight a book again!

	justice: punishment, deterrence, incapacitation, and rehabilitation.
Simmel	Simmel pioneered the concept of social structure. His most famous work today is probably "The Philosophy of Money".
Social conflict	Social conflict is a conflict or confrontation of social powers. Sociologist however differ in views whether social conflict is limited to hostile or antagonistic opposition and whether it is a clash of coercive powers or of any opposing social powers.
Criminalization	Criminalization refers to the process whereby criminal law is selectively applied to social behavior. It involves the enactment of legislation that outlaws certain types of behavior and provides for surveillance and policing of that behavior and whether or not the behavior is detected.
Authority	Authority refers to power that is attached to a position that others perceive as legitimate.
Organization	In sociology organization is understood as planned, coordinated and purposeful action of human beings to construct or compile a common tangible or intangible product or service.
Interest group	Interest group refers to an organization that attempts to affect political decisions by supporting candidates sympathetic to their interests and by influencing those already in positions of authority.
Differential Association	In criminology, Differential Association is a theory developed by Edwin Sutherland proposing that through interaction with others, individuals learn the values, attitudes, techniques, and motives for criminal behavior.
Neighborhood	A neighborhood is a geographically localized community located within a larger city, town or suburb. Traditionally, a neighborhood is small enough that the neighbors are all able to know each other.
Community	Community refers to a group of people who share a common sense of identity and interact with one another on a sustained basis.
Prejudice	Prejudice is, as the name implies, the process of "pre-judging" something. It implies coming to a judgment on a subject before learning where the preponderance of evidence actually lies, or forming a judgment without direct experience.
Social construction of reality	The process by which our perception of reality is shaped largely by the subjective meaning that we give to an experience is a social construction of reality.
Social construction	A social construction is an institutionalized entity or artifact in a social system 'invented' or 'constructed' by participants in a particular culture or society that exists solely because people agree to behave as if it exists, or agree to follow certain conventional rules.
Punishment	Punishment is the practice of imposing something unpleasant on a subject as a response to some unwanted behavior or disobedience that the subject has displayed.
Wright	Wright is an American sociologist. His work is concerned mainly with the study of social classes, and in particular with the task of providing an update to the Marxist concept of class. Wright has stressed the importance of the control of the means of production in defining 'class', while at the same trying to account for the situation of skilled employees, taking inspiration from Weberian accounts of authority.
Berger	Berger is perhaps best known for his view that social reality is a form of consciousness. Central to his work is the relationship between society and the individual. In his book The Social Construction of Reality Berger develops a sociological theory: 'Society as Objective Reality and as Subjective Reality'. His analysis of society as subjective reality describes

Go to **Cram101.com** for the Practice Tests for this Chapter.

Go to **Cram101.com** for the Practice Tests for this Chapter.
And, **NEVER** highlight a book again!

the process by which an individual's conception of reality is produced by his or her interaction with social structures.

Donald Black	Donald Black is author of the 1976 book The Behavior of Law, which has received very favorable reviews, and The Social Structure of Right and Wrong, which applies sociological concepts first explored in The Behavior of Law to subjects other than law, such as Right and Wrong, Crime as Social Control, Conflict Management, art, ideas (as an empirical distributed phenomenon), and God.
Social control	A social mechanism that regulates individual and group behavior through sanctions and rewards is a social control.
Division of labor	Division of labor is the specialisation of cooperative labor in specific, circumscribed tasks and roles, intended to increase efficiency of output.
Deviant behavior	Deviant behavior is behavior that is a recognized violation of social norms. Formal and informal social controls attempt to prevent and minimize deviance. One such control is through the medicalization of deviance.
Bureaucracy	Bureaucracy refers to a formal organization marked by a clear hierarchy of authority, the existence of written rules of procedure, staffed by full-time salaried officials, and striving for the efficient attainment of organizational goals.
Sanction	A punishment for nonconformity that reinforces socially approved forms of behavior is a sanction.
Social status	Social status refers to a position in a social relationship, a characteristic that locates individuals in relation to other people and sets of role expectations.
Mean	In statistics, mean has two related meanings: a)the average in ordinary English, which is also called the arithmetic mean (and is distinguished from the geometric mean or harmonic mean). The average is also called sample mean. b)the expected value of a random variable, which is also called the population mean.
Sociology of law	Sociology of law is also often conceived of as an approach within legal studies stressing the actual social effects of legal institutions, doctrines, and practices and vice versa. In the latter sense it is also referred to as the "law and society" approach, or even broader as "socio-legal studies".
Criminologist	A criminologist is often defined as someone who studies the aetiology of crime, criminal behavior, types of crime, and social, cultural and media reactions to crime.
Social forces	Social forces are the typical basic drives, or motives, which lead to the fundamental types of association and group relationship.
Conflict criminology	Largely based on the writings of Karl Marx, conflict criminology claims that crime is inevitable in capitalist societies, as invariably certain groups will become marginalized and unequal. In seeking equality, members of these groups may often turn to crime in order to gain the material wealth that apparently brings equality in capitalist economic states.
Jurisdiction	Jurisdiction refers to every kind of judicial action; the authority of courts and judicial officers to decide cases.
Variable	A characteristic that varies in value or magnitude along which an object, individual or group may be categorized, such as income or age, is referred to as a variable.
Social problem	A social condition that is perceived as having harmful effects is a social problem. Opinions about whether a condition is a social problem vary among groups and depend upon how and by whom the condition is defined and perceived in society.
Conflict model	The conflict model (non-System perspective or system conflict theory) of criminal justice

Go to **Cram101.com** for the Practice Tests for this Chapter.

argues that the organizations of a criminal justice system either do, or should, work competitively to produce justice, as opposed to cooperatively.

Social class	A category of people who occupy a similar position in relation to the means through which goods and services are produced in a society is a social class.
Discrimination	Discrimination refers to the denial of equal access to social resources to people on the basis of their group membership.
Mandatory sentence	A criminal sentence that is defined by a statutory requirement that states the penalty to be set for all cases of a specific offense is called a mandatory sentence.
Cocaine	Cocaine is a crystalline tropane alkaloid that is obtained from the leaves of the coca plant. It is a stimulant of the central nervous system and an appetite suppressant, creating what has been described as a euphoric sense of happiness and increased energy.
Violent crime	A violent crime or crime of violence is a crime in which the offender uses or threatens to use violent force upon the victim. The United States Department of Justice Bureau of Justice Statistics (BJS) counts five categories of crime as violent crimes: murder, rape, robbery, aggravated assault, and simple assault.
Critical criminology	Critical criminology rests upon the fundamental assertion that definitions of what constitute crimes are socially and historically contingent, that is, what constitutes a crime varies in different social situations and different periods of history.
Control theory	A theory that views crime as the outcome of an imbalance between impulses toward criminal activity and controls that deter it is referred to as control theory. Control theorists hold that criminals are rational beings who will act to maximize their own reward.
Aggregate	Aggregate refers to a collection of people who happen to be in the same place at the same time.
Bonding	In the social sciences, the concept of bonding refers to the formation of interpersonal relationships. Development of emotional attachment between the mother and newborn immediately after birth is considered bonding.
Government	A government is a body that has the authority to make and the power to enforce laws within a civil, corporate, religious, academic, or other organization or group.

Go to **Cram101.com** for the Practice Tests for this Chapter.
And, **NEVER** highlight a book again!

Critical theory	Critical theory is social theory oriented toward critiquing and changing society as a whole, in contrast to traditional theory oriented only to understanding or explaining it.
Conflict theory	Conflict theory or conflict perspective refers to a theory that conflict is normal and that the task is not to eliminate conflict but to learn to control it so that it becomes constructive.
Crime	Crime refers to any action that violates criminal laws established by political authority. A crime in a nontechnical sense is an act that violates a very important political or moral command.
Critical criminology	Critical criminology rests upon the fundamental assertion that definitions of what constitute crimes are socially and historically contingent, that is, what constitutes a crime varies in different social situations and different periods of history.
Means of production	Means of production are the materials, tools and other instruments used by workers to make products. This includes: machines, tools materials, plant and equipment, land, raw materials, money, power generation, and so on: anything necessary for labor to produce.
Criminal justice	Criminal justice refers to the system used by government to maintain social control, enforce laws, and administer justice. Law enforcement (police), courts, and corrections are the primary agencies charged with these responsibilities.
Social justice	Social justice refers to conceptions of justice applied to an entire society. It is based on the idea of a just society, which gives individuals and groups fair treatment and a just share of the benefits of society.
Criminology	Criminology refers to the systematic study of crime and the criminal justice system, including the police, courts, and prisons.
Mean	In statistics, mean has two related meanings: a)the average in ordinary English, which is also called the arithmetic mean (and is distinguished from the geometric mean or harmonic mean). The average is also called sample mean. b)the expected value of a random variable, which is also called the population mean.
Society	A society is a grouping of individuals, which is characterized by common interest and may have distinctive culture and institutions.
Industrial revolution	Industrial Revolution refers to the massive social, economic, and technological change in 18th and 19th century Great Britian. It commenced with the advent of the steam engine. Spread throughout Western Europe and North America in the 19th century.
Social change	Social change refers to alteration in social structures or culture over time.
Marx	Marx was an immensely influential German philosopher, political economist, and socialist revolutionary. While Marx addressed a wide range of issues, he is most famous for his analysis of history in terms of class struggles, summed up in the opening line of the introduction to the Communist Manifesto: "The history of all hitherto existing society is the history of class struggles."
Economic development	Economic development is the development of the economic wealth of countries or regions for the well-being of their inhabitants. Economic development is a sustainable increase in living standards that implies increased per capita income, better education and health as well as environmental protection.
Conflict criminology	Largely based on the writings of Karl Marx, conflict criminology claims that crime is inevitable in capitalist societies, as invariably certain groups will become marginalized and unequal. In seeking equality, members of these groups may often turn to crime in order to gain the material wealth that apparently brings equality in capitalist economic states.

Go to **Cram101.com** for the Practice Tests for this Chapter.
And, **NEVER** highlight a book again!

Social theory	Social theory refers to the use of theoretical frameworks to explain and analyze social patterns and large-scale social structures. Social theory attempts to answer the question 'what is?', not 'what should be?'. One should therefore not confuse it with philosophy or with belief.
Consensus	Agreement on basic social values by the members of a group or society is referred to as a consensus.
Capitalism	Capitalism is an economic system in which the means of production are owned mostly privately, and capital is invested in the production, distribution and other trade of goods and services, for profit in a competitive free market.
Marxism	Marxism refers to the philosophy and social theory based on Karl Marx's work on one hand, and to the political practice based on Marxist theory on the other hand (namely, parts of the First International during Marx's time, communist parties and later states).
Relations of production	Relations of production is a concept frequently used by Karl Marx in his theory of historical materialism and in Das Kapital. Beyond examining specific cases, Marx never defined the general concept exactly however. It is evident though that it refers to all kinds of social and technical human interconnections involved in the social production and reproduction of material life.
Forces of production	Marx's term to refer to the combination of the means of production with human labor power is forces of production.
Social relation	Social relation can refer to a multitude of social interactions, regulated by social norms, between two or more people, with each having a social position and performing a social role.
Material good	In economics and philosophy, a material good is a good that can be purchased or sold and from which one receives non-spiritual pleasure.
Organization	In sociology organization is understood as planned, coordinated and purposeful action of human beings to construct or compile a common tangible or intangible product or service.
Technology	The application of logic, reason and knowledge to the problems of exploiting raw materials from the environment, is referred to as a technology.
Feudalism	Feudalism refers to a general set of reciprocal legal and military obligations among the warrior nobility of Europe during the Middle Ages, revolving around the three key concepts of lords, vassals, and fiefs.
Socialism	Socialism refers to a broad array of doctrines or political movements that envisage a socio-economic system in which property and the distribution of wealth are subject to social control.
Depression	In the field of psychiatry, the word depression can also have this meaning of low mood but more specifically refers to a mental illness when it has reached a severity and duration to warrant a diagnosis, whether there is an obvious situational cause or not.
Criminal law	Criminal law (also known as penal law) is the body of statutory and common law that deals with crime and the legal punishment of criminal offenses. There are four theories of criminal justice: punishment, deterrence, incapacitation, and rehabilitation.
Lumpenproletariat	The lumpenproletariat is a term originally defined by Marx and Engels in The German Ideology which refers to the 'refuse of all classes'.
Social contract	The theory of the social contract is based on the assumption that all men live in a state of nature which is not ideal. In order to move away from these conditions men enter into a contract with each other, allowing them to live in peace and unity. The theory of the social contract can be seen as a justification for the formation of the state.

Go to **Cram101.com** for the Practice Tests for this Chapter.
And, **NEVER** highlight a book again!

Social order	Social order refers to a set of linked social structures, social institutions and social practices which conserve, maintain and enforce "normal" ways of relating and behaving.
Rebellion	A rebellion is, in the most general sense, a refusal to accept authority. It may therefore be seen as encompassing a range of behaviors from civil disobedience to a violent organized attempt to destroy established authority. It is often used in reference to armed resistance against an established government, but can also refer to mass nonviolent resistance movements.
New criminology	A branch of criminological thought, prominent in Britain in the 1970s, that regarded deviance as deliberately chosen and often political in nature. New criminology argued that crime and deviance could only be understood in the context of power.
Taylor	Taylor was an American engineer who sought to improve industrial efficiency. He was one of the intellectual leaders of the Efficiency Movement and his ideas, broadly conceived, were highly influential in the Progressive Era. During the latter part of his career he was a management consultant, and he is sometimes called "The Father of Scientific Management."
Engels	Engels developed communist theory alongside his better-known collaborator, Karl Marx, co-authoring The Communist Manifesto (1848). Engels also edited several volumes of Das Kapital after Marx's death.
Ideology	Ideology refers to shared ideas or beliefs which serve to justify and support the interests of a particular group or organizations.
Working class	Working class refers to a social class of industrial societies broadly composed of people involved in manual occupation.
Marxist criminology	Marxist criminology is one of the schools of criminology. It parallels the work of the functionalist school which focuses on what produces stability and continuity in society but, unlike the functionalists, it adopts a predefined political philosophy.
Criminologist	A criminologist is often defined as someone who studies the aetiology of crime, criminal behavior, types of crime, and social, cultural and media reactions to crime.
Bias	A bias is a prejudice in a general or specific sense, usually in the sense for having a preference to one particular point of view or ideological perspective.
Ruling class	The term ruling class refers to the social class of a given society that decides upon and sets that society's political policy.
Community	Community refers to a group of people who share a common sense of identity and interact with one another on a sustained basis.
Punishment	Punishment is the practice of imposing something unpleasant on a subject as a response to some unwanted behavior or disobedience that the subject has displayed.
Political economy	The social arrangements through which political and economic institutions support each other is a political economy.
Range	A measure of variability defined as the high score in a distribution minus the low score is referred to as a range.
Deviant behavior	Deviant behavior is behavior that is a recognized violation of social norms. Formal and informal social controls attempt to prevent and minimize deviance. One such control is through the medicalization of deviance.
Criminalization	Criminalization refers to the process whereby criminal law is selectively applied to social behavior. It involves the enactment of legislation that outlaws certain types of behavior and provides for surveillance and policing of that behavior and whether or not the behavior is detected.

Go to **Cram101.com** for the Practice Tests for this Chapter.
And, **NEVER** highlight a book again!

Strain theory	The proposition that people feel strain when they are exposed to cultural goals that they are unable to obtain because they do not have access to culturally approved means of achieving those goals is strain theory.
Organized crime	Organized crime is crime carried out systematically by formal criminal organizations.
Social problem	A social condition that is perceived as having harmful effects is a social problem. Opinions about whether a condition is a social problem vary among groups and depend upon how and by whom the condition is defined and perceived in society.
Political system	A political system or political institution is a social system of politics and government. It is usually compared to the law system, economic system, cultural system, and other social systems.
Decriminaliz-tion	The removal of criminal prohibitions for certain behaviors while still regulating them is decriminalization.
Contradiction	Marx's term to refer to mutually antagonistic tendencies within institutions or the broader society such as those between profit and competition within capitalism is referred to as a contradiction.
Alienation	In sociology and critical social theory, alienation refers to the individual's estrangement from traditional community and others in general.
Modernism	Modernism is a trend of thought which affirms the power of human beings to make, improve and reshape their environment, with the aid of scientific knowledge, technology and practical experimentation.
Retreatism	A form of deviance in which a person withdraws from social life by rejecting values and norms without offering alternatives is referred to as retreatism.
Sociology of law	Sociology of law is also often conceived of as an approach within legal studies stressing the actual social effects of legal institutions, doctrines, and practices and vice versa. In the latter sense it is also referred to as the "law and society" approach, or even broader as "socio-legal studies".
Postmodernism	The belief that society is no longer governed by history or progress, in which postmodern society is highly pluralistic and diverse, with no grand narrative guiding its development, is referred to as postmodernism.
Modernity	Modernity is a term used to describe the condition of being "Modern". Modernity is often characterized by comparing modern societies to premodern or postmodern ones, and the understanding of those non-modern social statuses is, again, far from a settled issue.
Bureaucracy	Bureaucracy refers to a formal organization marked by a clear hierarchy of authority, the existence of written rules of procedure, staffed by full-time salaried officials, and striving for the efficient attainment of organizational goals.
Social position	The social identity an individual has in a given group or society, where social positions may be general in nature or may be more specific, is referred to as a social position.
Discourse	In the social sciences, a discourse is considered to be an institutionalized way of thinking, a social boundary defining what can be said about a specific topic.
Constitutive criminology	The most thoroughgoing postmodern perspective in criminology and it is a political perspective that seeks to lay bare the rhetoric and mystification that enters public discourse about crime is a constitutive criminology.
Frame of reference	One's unique patterning of perceptions and attitudes according to which one evaluates and reacts to events is a frame of reference.

Go to **Cram101.com** for the Practice Tests for this Chapter.

Go to **Cram101.com** for the Practice Tests for this Chapter.
And, **NEVER** highlight a book again!

Gang	A gang is a group of individuals who share a common identity and, in current usage, engage in illegal activities. Historically the term referred to both criminal groups and ordinary groups of friends.
Social policy	Social policy relates to guidelines for the changing, maintenance or creation of living conditions that are conducive to human welfare. Thus social policy is that part of public policy that has to do with social issues such as public access to social programs.
Crime rate	Crime rate is a measure of the rate of occurrence of crimes committed in a given area and time. Most commonly, crime rate is given as the number of crimes committed among a given number of persons.
Dominance	In animal colonies, a condition established by one animal over another by prevailing in an aggressive encounter between the two, is referred to as dominance.
Relativism	Relativism expresses the view that the meaning and value of human beliefs and behaviors have no absolute reference.
Validity	The degree to which a measurement instrument measures what it is intended to measure is referred to as validity.

Go to **Cram101.com** for the Practice Tests for this Chapter.

Go to **Cram101.com** for the Practice Tests for this Chapter.
And, **NEVER** highlight a book again!

Criminology	Criminology refers to the systematic study of crime and the criminal justice system, including the police, courts, and prisons.
Feminism	Feminism is a diverse collection of social theories, political movements and moral philosophies, largely motivated by or concerned with the experiences of women.
Crime	Crime refers to any action that violates criminal laws established by political authority. A crime in a nontechnical sense is an act that violates a very important political or moral command.
Gender	Gender refers to socially defined behavior regarded as appropriate for the members of each
Patriarchy	Patriarchy is the anthropological term used to define the sociological condition where male members of a society tend to predominate in positions of power; with the more powerful the position, the more likely it is that a male will hold that position.
Capitalism	Capitalism is an economic system in which the means of production are owned mostly privately, and capital is invested in the production, distribution and other trade of goods and services, for profit in a competitive free market.
Violent crime	A violent crime or crime of violence is a crime in which the offender uses or threatens to use violent force upon the victim. The United States Department of Justice Bureau of Justice Statistics (BJS) counts five categories of crime as violent crimes: murder, rape, robbery, aggravated assault, and simple assault.
Social role	A social role is a set of connected behaviors, rights and obligations as conceptualized by actors in a social situation. It is mostly defined as an expected behavior in a given individual social status and social position.
Criminal justice	Criminal justice refers to the system used by government to maintain social control, enforce laws, and administer justice. Law enforcement (police), courts, and corrections are the primary agencies charged with these responsibilities.
Punishment	Punishment is the practice of imposing something unpleasant on a subject as a response to some unwanted behavior or disobedience that the subject has displayed.
Criminologist	A criminologist is often defined as someone who studies the aetiology of crime, criminal behavior, types of crime, and social, cultural and media reactions to crime.
Validity	The degree to which a measurement instrument measures what it is intended to measure is referred to as validity.
Range	A measure of variability defined as the high score in a distribution minus the low score is referred to as a range.
Social structure	The term social structure, used in a general sense, refers to entities or groups in definite relation to each other, to relatively enduring patterns of behavior and relationship within social systems, or to social institutions and norms becoming embedded into social systems in such a way that they shape the behavior of actors within those social systems.
Liberal feminism	A branch of feminism that argues that gender equality can he achieved without challenging men as a group or changing basic economic and political arrangements such as capitalism is a liberal feminism.
Society	A society is a grouping of individuals, which is characterized by common interest and may have distinctive culture and institutions.
Social relation	Social relation can refer to a multitude of social interactions, regulated by social norms, between two or more people, with each having a social position and performing a social role.
Feudalism	Feudalism refers to a general set of reciprocal legal and military obligations among the

Go to **Cram101.com** for the Practice Tests for this Chapter.
And, **NEVER** highlight a book again!

warrior nobility of Europe during the Middle Ages, revolving around the three key concepts of lords, vassals, and fiefs.

Organization	In sociology organization is understood as planned, coordinated and purposeful action of human beings to construct or compile a common tangible or intangible product or service.
Gender identity	Gender identity describes the gender with which a person identifies, but can also be used to refer to the gender that other people attribute to the individual on the basis of what they know from gender role indications
Socialization	Socialization refers to the lifelong processes through which humans develop an awareness of social norms and values, and achieve a distinct sense of self.
Radical feminism	A branch of feminism that argues that patriarchy centers on a fundamental difference in interests between men and women, and that equality for women cannot be achieved unless men collectively give up the power, wealth, and privilege that patriarchy grants them, is referred to as radical feminism.
Dominance	In animal colonies, a condition established by one animal over another by prevailing in an aggressive encounter between the two, is referred to as dominance.
Marxism	Marxism refers to the philosophy and social theory based on Karl Marx's work on one hand, and to the political practice based on Marxist theory on the other hand (namely, parts of the First International during Marx's time, communist parties and later states).
Mean	In statistics, mean has two related meanings: a)the average in ordinary English, which is also called the arithmetic mean (and is distinguished from the geometric mean or harmonic mean). The average is also called sample mean. b)the expected value of a random variable, which is also called the population mean.
Marxist criminology	Marxist criminology is one of the schools of criminology. It parallels the work of the functionalist school which focuses on what produces stability and continuity in society but, unlike the functionalists, it adopts a predefined political philosophy.
Criminal law	Criminal law (also known as penal law) is the body of statutory and common law that deals with crime and the legal punishment of criminal offenses. There are four theories of criminal justice: punishment, deterrence, incapacitation, and rehabilitation.
Feminist theory	Theory or perspective that focuses on male dominance in families and society and examines how gender differences are related to power differentials between men and women is a feminist theory.
Birth control	Birth control is a regimen of one or more actions, devices, or medications followed in order to deliberately prevent or reduce the likelihood of a woman giving birth or becoming pregnant.
Sexual division of labor	The assignment of different work tasks to men and women is called sexual division of labor.
Division of labor	Division of labor is the specialisation of cooperative labor in specific, circumscribed tasks and roles, intended to increase efficiency of output.
Postmodernism	The belief that society is no longer governed by history or progress, in which postmodern society is highly pluralistic and diverse, with no grand narrative guiding its development, is referred to as postmodernism.
Social justice	Social justice refers to conceptions of justice applied to an entire society. It is based on the idea of a just society, which gives individuals and groups fair treatment and a just share of the benefits of society.
Paradigm	In social science, paradigm is used to describe the set of experiences, beliefs and values

Go to **Cram101.com** for the Practice Tests for this Chapter.
And, **NEVER** highlight a book again!

that affect the way an individual perceives reality and responds to that perception.

Relativism	Relativism expresses the view that the meaning and value of human beliefs and behaviors have no absolute reference.
Generalizability	Generalizability refers to ability to extend a set of findings observed in one piece of research to a larger population or group than the group being studied.
Empirical research	Empirical research is any research that bases its findings on direct or indirect observation as its test of reality. Such research may also be conducted according to hypothetico-deductive procedures, such as those developed from the work of R. A. Fisher.
Case Study	Case study refers to a research design that focuses on a single example rather than a representative sample.
Social class	A category of people who occupy a similar position in relation to the means through which goods and services are produced in a society is a social class.
Direct relationship	In mathematics and statistics, a positive or direct relationship is a relationship between two variables in which they both increase or decrease in conjunction.
Patriarchal family	Patriarchal family refers to a family in which the father is head of the household with authority over other family members.
Gender role	A gender role is a set of behavioral norms associated with males and with females, respectively, in a given social group or system.
Conformity	Conformity is the act of consciously maintaining a certain degree of similarity (in clothing, manners, behaviors, etc.) to those in your general social circles, to those in authority, or to the general status quo. Usually, conformity implies a tendency to submit to others in thought and behavior other than simply clothing choice.
Differential Association	In criminology, Differential Association is a theory developed by Edwin Sutherland proposing that through interaction with others, individuals learn the values, attitudes, techniques, and motives for criminal behavior.
Control balance	Control balance refers to a theory claiming that the amount of control to which an individual is subject, relative to the amount of control she/he can exercise, determines the probability of deviance occurring as well as the likely type of deviance.
Victimizations	Victimizations refer to the number of people who are victims of criminal acts; young teens are fifteen times more likely than older adults to be victims of crimes.
Sanction	A punishment for nonconformity that reinforces socially approved forms of behavior is a sanction.
Femininity	Femininity comprises the physical and mental attributes associated with the female sex and is partly culturally determined.
Masculinity	Masculinity refers to the characteristic forms of behavior expected of men in any given culture.
Robbery	The unlawful taking of, or the attempt to take something of value from another person or persons by using violence or the threat of violence, is referred to as a robbery.
Caste	Caste refers to a closed form of stratification in which an individual's status is determined by birth and cannot be changed.
Variable	A characteristic that varies in value or magnitude along which an object, individual or group may be categorized, such as income or age, is referred to as a variable.
Peer group	A friendship group with common interests and position composed of individuals of similar age

Go to **Cram101.com** for the Practice Tests for this Chapter.

Go to **Cram101.com** for the Practice Tests for this Chapter.
And, **NEVER** highlight a book again!

is referred to as a peer group.

Gang   A gang is a group of individuals who share a common identity and, in current usage, engage in illegal activities. Historically the term referred to both criminal groups and ordinary groups of friends.

Strain theory   The proposition that people feel strain when they are exposed to cultural goals that they are unable to obtain because they do not have access to culturally approved means of achieving those goals is strain theory.

Crime rate   Crime rate is a measure of the rate of occurrence of crimes committed in a given area and time. Most commonly, crime rate is given as the number of crimes committed among a given number of persons.

Social issue   Social issue refers to matters that can be explained only by factors outside an individual's control and immediate social environment. They usually concern more than a single individual and affect many individuals in a society.

Sexual abuse   Sexual abuse is defined by the forcing of undesired sexual acts by one person to another.

Go to **Cram101.com** for the Practice Tests for this Chapter.
And, **NEVER** highlight a book again!

Developmental theories	Those that assert that personal characteristics guide human development and influence behavioral choices but that these choices may change over the life course are called developmental theories.
Crime	Crime refers to any action that violates criminal laws established by political authority. A crime in a nontechnical sense is an act that violates a very important political or moral command.
Criminology	Criminology refers to the systematic study of crime and the criminal justice system, including the police, courts, and prisons.
Felony	The term felony is used for very serious crimes, whereas misdemeanors are considered to be less serious offenses. It is a crime punishable by one or more years of imprisonment.
Crime rate	Crime rate is a measure of the rate of occurrence of crimes committed in a given area and time. Most commonly, crime rate is given as the number of crimes committed among a given number of persons.
Frequency	In statistics the frequency of an event i is the number n_i of times the event occurred in the experiment or the study.
Cohort	A cohort is a group of subjects, most often humans from a given population, defined by experiencing an event (typically birth) in a particular time span.
Cohort study	Cohort study refers to a study in which some specific subpopulation or cohort is studied over time, although data may be collected from different members in each set of observations.
Public policy	Public policy is a course of action or inaction chosen by public authorities to address a problem. Public policy is expressed in the body of laws, regulations, decisions and actions of government.
Criminal law	Criminal law (also known as penal law) is the body of statutory and common law that deals with crime and the legal punishment of criminal offenses. There are four theories of criminal justice: punishment, deterrence, incapacitation, and rehabilitation.
Paradigm	In social science, paradigm is used to describe the set of experiences, beliefs and values that affect the way an individual perceives reality and responds to that perception.
Aggregate	Aggregate refers to a collection of people who happen to be in the same place at the same time.
Burglary	Burglary – also called breaking and entering or house breaking – is a crime related to theft. It typically involves someone breaking into a house with an intent to commit a crime.
Criminologist	A criminologist is often defined as someone who studies the aetiology of crime, criminal behavior, types of crime, and social, cultural and media reactions to crime.
Criminal justice	Criminal justice refers to the system used by government to maintain social control, enforce laws, and administer justice. Law enforcement (police), courts, and corrections are the primary agencies charged with these responsibilities.
Juvenile delinquency	Juvenile delinquency refers to antisocial or criminal acts performed by minors. It is an important social issue because juveniles are capable of committing serious crimes, but most legal systems prescribe specific procedures and punishments for dealing with such crimes.
Variable	A characteristic that varies in value or magnitude along which an object, individual or group may be categorized, such as income or age, is referred to as a variable.
Violent crime	A violent crime or crime of violence is a crime in which the offender uses or threatens to use violent force upon the victim. The United States Department of Justice Bureau of Justice Statistics (BJS) counts five categories of crime as violent crimes: murder, rape, robbery,

Go to **Cram101.com** for the Practice Tests for this Chapter.

117

	aggravated assault, and simple assault.
Longitudinal study	A type of developmental study in which the same group of participants is followed and measured at different ages is a longitudinal study.
Interactional theory	Interactional theory asserts that youths' interactions with institutions and events over the life course determine criminal behavior patterns and that these patterns of behavior evolve over time.
Social constraint	Social constraint refers to the conditioning influence of the groups and societies of which we are a part on our behavior. Social constraint was regarded by Emile Durkheim as one of the distinctive properties of social facts.
Control theory	A theory that views crime as the outcome of an imbalance between impulses toward criminal activity and controls that deter it is referred to as control theory. Control theorists hold that criminals are rational beings who will act to maximize their own reward.
Social learning theory	A theory emphasizing that boys develop maleness and girls develop femaleness through exposure to scores of influence-including parents, peers, television, and schools-that teach them what it means to be a man or a woman in their culture, is referred to as a social learning theory.
Social learning	The process through which we acquire new information, forms of behavior, or attitudes exclusively or primarily in a social group, is referred to as a social learning.
Late adolescence	Late adolescence refers to approximately the latter half of the second decade of life. Career interests, dating, and identity exploration are often more pronounced in late adolescence than in early adolescence.
Adolescence	Adolescence is the transitional stage of human development in which a juvenile matures into an adult. This transition involves biological (i.e. pubertal), social, and psychological changes, though the biological ones are the easiest to measure objectively.
Convention	A convention is a set of agreed, stipulated or generally accepted social norms, norms, standards or criteria, often taking the form of a custom.
Society	A society is a grouping of individuals, which is characterized by common interest and may have distinctive culture and institutions.
Causal Relationship	A relationship in which one state of affairs is brought about by another is defined as a causal relationship.
Social control	A social mechanism that regulates individual and group behavior through sanctions and rewards is a social control.
Family disruption	Family disruption refers to the behaviors associated with altering or terminating family and pseudo-family units; separation, annulment, divorce, disownment, death, etc.
Mean	In statistics, mean has two related meanings: a)the average in ordinary English, which is also called the arithmetic mean (and is distinguished from the geometric mean or harmonic mean). The average is also called sample mean. b)the expected value of a random variable, which is also called the population mean.
Social bond	Social bond refers to ties a person to the institutions and processes of society; elements of the bond include attachment, commitment, involvement, and belief.
Crime prevention	Crime prevention is a term describing techniques used in reducing victimization as well as deterring crime and criminals. It is applied specifically to efforts made by governments to reduce crime and law enforcement and criminal justice.
Social class	A category of people who occupy a similar position in relation to the means through which goods and services are produced in a society is a social class.

Go to **Cram101.com** for the Practice Tests for this Chapter.

Go to **Cram101.com** for the Practice Tests for this Chapter.
And, **NEVER** highlight a book again!

Social capital	Social capital is defined as the advantage created by a person's location in a structure of relationships. It explains how some people gain more success in a particular setting through their superior connections to other people. There are in fact a variety of inter-related definitions of this term, which has been described as "something of a cure-all" (Portes, 1998) for all the problems afflicting communities and societies today.
Human capital	Human capital is a way of defining and categorizing peoples' skills and abilities as used in employment and as they otherwise contribute to the economy. Many early economic theories refer to it simply as labor, one of three factors of production, and consider it to be a commodity.
Coleman	Coleman was a sociological theorist, who studied the sociology of education, public policy, and was one of the earliest users of the term "social capital". His Foundations of Social Theory stands as one of the most important sociological contributions of the late-20th century.

Go to **Cram101.com** for the Practice Tests for this Chapter.

121

Criminologist	A criminologist is often defined as someone who studies the aetiology of crime, criminal behavior, types of crime, and social, cultural and media reactions to crime.
Criminology	Criminology refers to the systematic study of crime and the criminal justice system, including the police, courts, and prisons.
Crime	Crime refers to any action that violates criminal laws established by political authority. A crime in a nontechnical sense is an act that violates a very important political or moral command.
Social learning	The process through which we acquire new information, forms of behavior, or attitudes exclusively or primarily in a social group, is referred to as a social learning.
Social learning theory	A theory emphasizing that boys develop maleness and girls develop femaleness through exposure to scores of influence-including parents, peers, television, and schools-that teach them what it means to be a man or a woman in their culture, is referred to as a social learning theory.
Social Control Theory	In criminology, Social Control Theory as represented in the work of Travis Hirschi fits into the Positivist School, Neo-Classical School, and, later, Right Realism. It proposes that exploiting the process of socialization and social learning builds self-control and reduces the inclination to indulge in behavior recognized as antisocial.
Social control	A social mechanism that regulates individual and group behavior through sanctions and rewards is a social control.
Control theory	A theory that views crime as the outcome of an imbalance between impulses toward criminal activity and controls that deter it is referred to as control theory. Control theorists hold that criminals are rational beings who will act to maximize their own reward.
Strain theory	The proposition that people feel strain when they are exposed to cultural goals that they are unable to obtain because they do not have access to culturally approved means of achieving those goals is strain theory.
Society	A society is a grouping of individuals, which is characterized by common interest and may have distinctive culture and institutions.
Social disorganization	Social disorganization refers to a structural condition of society caused by rapid change in social institutions, norms, and values.
Socialization	Socialization refers to the lifelong processes through which humans develop an awareness of social norms and values, and achieve a distinct sense of self.
Community	Community refers to a group of people who share a common sense of identity and interact with one another on a sustained basis.
Punishment	Punishment is the practice of imposing something unpleasant on a subject as a response to some unwanted behavior or disobedience that the subject has displayed.
Deviant behavior	Deviant behavior is behavior that is a recognized violation of social norms. Formal and informal social controls attempt to prevent and minimize deviance. One such control is through the medicalization of deviance.
Peer group	A friendship group with common interests and position composed of individuals of similar age is referred to as a peer group.
Conformity	Conformity is the act of consciously maintaining a certain degree of similarity (in clothing, manners, behaviors, etc.) to those in your general social circles, to those in authority, or to the general status quo. Usually, conformity implies a tendency to submit to others in thought and behavior other than simply clothing choice.
Social group	A group that consists of two or more people who interact frequently and share a common

Go to **Cram101.com** for the Practice Tests for this Chapter.

Go to **Cram101.com** for the Practice Tests for this Chapter.
And, **NEVER** highlight a book again!

	identity and a feeling of interdependence, is referred to as a social group.
Bonding	In the social sciences, the concept of bonding refers to the formation of interpersonal relationships. Development of emotional attachment between the mother and newborn immediately after birth is considered bonding.
Differential Association	In criminology, Differential Association is a theory developed by Edwin Sutherland proposing that through interaction with others, individuals learn the values, attitudes, techniques, and motives for criminal behavior.
Labeling	Labeling is defining or describing a person in terms of his or her behavior. The term is often used in sociology to describe human interaction, control and identification of deviant behavior.
Crime rate	Crime rate is a measure of the rate of occurrence of crimes committed in a given area and time. Most commonly, crime rate is given as the number of crimes committed among a given number of persons.
Victimless crime	Victimless crime refers to violation of law in which there is no other person victimized, such as drug-taking or illegal gambling.
Deviant subculture	A subculture which has values and norms which differ substantially from those of the majority in a society is a deviant subculture.
Labeling theory	A social theory that holds that society's reaction to certain behaviors is a major factor in defining the self as deviant is labeling theory.
Stigmatized	People who have been negatively labeled because of their participation, or alleged participation, in deviant or outlawed behaviors are referred to as stigmatized.
Subculture	A group within the broader society that has values, norms and lifestyle distinct from those of the majority, is referred to as a subculture.
Social disorganization theory	Social disorganization theory argues that delinquency is a product of the social forces existing in inner-city, low-income areas.
Urbanization	Urbanization is the increase over time in the population of cities in relation to the region's rural population. Urbanization has intense effects on the ecology of a region and on its economy.
Illegitimate opportunity	Illegitimate opportunity theory holds that individuals commit crimes when the chances of being caught are low.
Consequent	Consequent refers to the second of two propositions in a logical argument of the form If antecedent is true, then consequent follows.
Compliance	Conforming behavior that occurs in response to direct social pressure is referred to as compliance.
Deterrence	Deterrence is a theory from behavioral psychology about preventing or controlling actions or behavior through fear of punishment or retribution. This theory of criminology is shaping the criminal justice system of the United States and various other countries.
Consensus	Agreement on basic social values by the members of a group or society is referred to as a consensus.
Restorative justice	Restorative justice is commonly known as a theory of criminal justice that focuses on crime as an act against another individual or community rather than the state. The victim plays a major role in the process and may receive some type of restitution from the offender.
Criminal justice	Criminal justice refers to the system used by government to maintain social control, enforce

Go to **Cram101.com** for the Practice Tests for this Chapter.

Go to **Cram101.com** for the Practice Tests for this Chapter.
And, **NEVER** highlight a book again!

laws, and administer justice. Law enforcement (police), courts, and corrections are the primary agencies charged with these responsibilities.

Routine activities theory	Routine activities theory claims that patterns of crime and victimization are the result of the everyday interaction of likely offenders, suitable targets, and guardians.
Control balance	Control balance refers to a theory claiming that the amount of control to which an individual is subject, relative to the amount of control she/he can exercise, determines the probability of deviance occurring as well as the likely type of deviance.
Balance Theory	Balance theory is a theoretical perspective on social interaction that suggests that people organize their perceptions of people and objects into units and strive for some consistency in the positive and negative feelings among them.
Merton	Merton coined the phrase "self-fulfilling prophecy." He also coined many other phrases that have gone into everyday use, such as "role model" and "unintended consequences".
Anomie	Durkheim's designation for a condition in which social control becomes ineffective as a result of the loss of shared values and a sense of purpose in society is defined as anomie.
Range	A measure of variability defined as the high score in a distribution minus the low score is referred to as a range.
Exploitation	In political economy, economics, and sociology, exploitation involves a persistent social relationship in which certain persons are being mistreated or unfairly used for the benefit of others. This corresponds to one ethical conception of exploitation, that is, the treatment of human beings as mere means to an end — or as mere "objects".
Robbery	The unlawful taking of, or the attempt to take something of value from another person or persons by using violence or the threat of violence, is referred to as a robbery.
Rape	Rape is the act of forcing penetrative sexual acts, against another's will through violence, force, threat of injury, or other duress, or where the victim is unable to decline, due to the effects of drugs or alcohol.
Norm	In sociology, a norm, or social norm, is a rule that is socially enforced. Social sanctioning is what distinguishes norms from other cultural products such as meaning and values.
Variable	A characteristic that varies in value or magnitude along which an object, individual or group may be categorized, such as income or age, is referred to as a variable.
Autonomy	Autonomy is a concept found in moral, political, and bioethical philosophy. Within these contexts it refers to the capacity of a rational individual to make an informed, uncoerced decision. In moral and political philosophy, autonomy is often used as the basis for determining moral responsibility for one's actions.
Paradigm	In social science, paradigm is used to describe the set of experiences, beliefs and values that affect the way an individual perceives reality and responds to that perception.
Embezzlement	Embezzlement is the fraudulent appropriation by a person to his own use of property or money entrusted to that person's care but owned by someone else.
Developmental theories	Those that assert that personal characteristics guide human development and influence behavioral choices but that these choices may change over the life course are called developmental theories.
Sexual assault	Sexual assault is any undesired physical contact of a sexual nature perpetrated against another person. While associated with rape, sexual assault is much broader and the specifics may vary according to social, political or legal definition.

Go to **Cram101.com** for the Practice Tests for this Chapter.

Go to **Cram101.com** for the Practice Tests for this Chapter.
And, **NEVER** highlight a book again!

Narcotic	A narcotic is an addictive drug, derived from opium, that reduces pain, induces sleep and may alter mood or behavior.
Political crime	A term used to describe illegal or unethical acts involving the usurpation of power by government officials or illegal or unethical acts perpetrated against the government by outsiders seeking to make a political statement or undermine the government, is referred to as a political crime.
Validity	The degree to which a measurement instrument measures what it is intended to measure is referred to as validity.
Statistical significance	The condition that exists when the probability that the observed findings are due to chance is very low is a statistical significance.
Dependent variable	A variable affected by another variable, is referred to as a dependent variable.

Go to **Cram101.com** for the Practice Tests for this Chapter.
And, **NEVER** highlight a book again!

Criminology	Criminology refers to the systematic study of crime and the criminal justice system, including the police, courts, and prisons.
Crime	Crime refers to any action that violates criminal laws established by political authority. A crime in a nontechnical sense is an act that violates a very important political or moral command.
Lewin	Lewin became one of the pioneers of social psychology. Often called "the father of social psychology," and one of the first researchers to study group dynamics and organizational development, he advocated Gestalt psychology.
Crime rate	Crime rate is a measure of the rate of occurrence of crimes committed in a given area and time. Most commonly, crime rate is given as the number of crimes committed among a given number of persons.
Unemployment rate	In economics, one who is willing to work at a prevailing wage rate yet is unable to find a paying job is considered to be unemployed. The unemployment rate is the number of unemployed workers divided by the total civilian labor force, which includes both the unemployed and those with jobs (all those willing and able to work for pay).
Community	Community refers to a group of people who share a common sense of identity and interact with one another on a sustained basis.
Violent crime	A violent crime or crime of violence is a crime in which the offender uses or threatens to use violent force upon the victim. The United States Department of Justice Bureau of Justice Statistics (BJS) counts five categories of crime as violent crimes: murder, rape, robbery, aggravated assault, and simple assault.
Variable	A characteristic that varies in value or magnitude along which an object, individual or group may be categorized, such as income or age, is referred to as a variable.
Adoption Study	Adoption study refers to a study in which investigators seek to discover whether, in behavior and psychological characteristics, adopted children are more like their adoptive parents, who provided a home environment, or more like their biological parents who contributed their home.
Causal Relationship	A relationship in which one state of affairs is brought about by another is defined as a causal relationship.
Range	A measure of variability defined as the high score in a distribution minus the low score is referred to as a range.
Interpersonal relationship	An interpersonal relationship is a social association, connection, or affiliation between two or more people. They vary in differing levels of intimacy and sharing, implying the discovery or establishment of common ground, and may be centered around something(s) shared in common.
Strain theory	The proposition that people feel strain when they are exposed to cultural goals that they are unable to obtain because they do not have access to culturally approved means of achieving those goals is strain theory.
Depression	In the field of psychiatry, the word depression can also have this meaning of low mood but more specifically refers to a mental illness when it has reached a severity and duration to warrant a diagnosis, whether there is an obvious situational cause or not.
Focal concerns	The value orientations of lower-class subculture that is characterized by a need for excitement, trouble, smartness, toughness, fate, and personal autonomy are referred to as focal concerns.
Subculture	A group within the broader society that has values, norms and lifestyle distinct from those of the majority, is referred to as a subculture.

Go to **Cram101.com** for the Practice Tests for this Chapter.

Go to **Cram101.com** for the Practice Tests for this Chapter.
And, **NEVER** highlight a book again!

Cognition	The term cognition is used in several loosely related ways to refer to a facility for the human-like processing of information, applying knowledge and changing preferences
Autonomy	Autonomy is a concept found in moral, political, and bioethical philosophy. Within these contexts it refers to the capacity of a rational individual to make an informed, uncoerced decision. In moral and political philosophy, autonomy is often used as the basis for determining moral responsibility for one's actions.
Control theory	A theory that views crime as the outcome of an imbalance between impulses toward criminal activity and controls that deter it is referred to as control theory. Control theorists hold that criminals are rational beings who will act to maximize their own reward.
Validity	The degree to which a measurement instrument measures what it is intended to measure is referred to as validity.
Deterrence	Deterrence is a theory from behavioral psychology about preventing or controlling actions or behavior through fear of punishment or retribution. This theory of criminology is shaping the criminal justice system of the United States and various other countries.
Gender	Gender refers to socially defined behavior regarded as appropriate for the members of each
Empathy	Empathy is commonly defined as one's ability to recognize, perceive and directly experientially feel the emotion of another. As the states of mind, beliefs, and desires of others are intertwined with their emotions, one with empathy for another may often be able to more effectively divine another's modes of thought and mood.
Dysfunction	Dysfunction refers to an institution's negative impact on the sociocultural system.
Punishment	Punishment is the practice of imposing something unpleasant on a subject as a response to some unwanted behavior or disobedience that the subject has displayed.
Modernization	The process of general social change brought about by the transition from an agrarian to an industrial mode of production, is referred to as modernization.
Social change	Social change refers to alteration in social structures or culture over time.
Normlessness	Emile Durkheim described anomie which is state of relative normlessness or a state in which norms have been eroded.
Durkheim	Durkheim sought to create one of the first scientific approaches to social phenomena. Along with Herbert Spencer, Durkheim was one of the first people to explain the existence and quality of different parts of a society by reference to what function they served in keeping the society healthy and balanced—a position that would come to be known as functionalism.
Society	A society is a grouping of individuals, which is characterized by common interest and may have distinctive culture and institutions.
Neighborhood	A neighborhood is a geographically localized community located within a larger city, town or suburb. Traditionally, a neighborhood is small enough that the neighbors are all able to know each other.
Mean	In statistics, mean has two related meanings: a)the average in ordinary English, which is also called the arithmetic mean (and is distinguished from the geometric mean or harmonic mean). The average is also called sample mean. b)the expected value of a random variable, which is also called the population mean.
Social structure	The term social structure, used in a general sense, refers to entities or groups in definite relation to each other, to relatively enduring patterns of behavior and relationship within social systems, or to social institutions and norms becoming embedded into social systems in such a way that they shape the behavior of actors within those social systems.

Go to **Cram101.com** for the Practice Tests for this Chapter.

Go to **Cram101.com** for the Practice Tests for this Chapter.
And, **NEVER** highlight a book again!

Social group	A group that consists of two or more people who interact frequently and share a common identity and a feeling of interdependence, is referred to as a social group.
Social status	Social status refers to a position in a social relationship, a characteristic that locates individuals in relation to other people and sets of role expectations.
Illegitimate opportunity structures	Circumstances that provide an opportunity for people to acquire through illegitimate activities what they cannot achieve through legitimate channels are illegitimate opportunity structures.
Illegitimate opportunity	Illegitimate opportunity theory holds that individuals commit crimes when the chances of being caught are low.
Opportunity structure	The distribution of opportunities to achieve goals in a social system is referred to as an opportunity structure.
Social disorganization	Social disorganization refers to a structural condition of society caused by rapid change in social institutions, norms, and values.
Economic development	Economic development is the development of the economic wealth of countries or regions for the well-being of their inhabitants. Economic development is a sustainable increase in living standards that implies increased per capita income, better education and health as well as environmental protection.
Family disruption	Family disruption refers to the behaviors associated with altering or terminating family and pseudo-family units; separation, annulment, divorce, disownment, death, etc.
Organization	In sociology organization is understood as planned, coordinated and purposeful action of human beings to construct or compile a common tangible or intangible product or service.
Rationalization	Rationalization is the process whereby an increasing number of social actions and interactions become based on considerations of efficiency or calculation rather than on motivations derived from custom, tradition, or emotion.
Social learning	The process through which we acquire new information, forms of behavior, or attitudes exclusively or primarily in a social group, is referred to as a social learning.
Control balance	Control balance refers to a theory claiming that the amount of control to which an individual is subject, relative to the amount of control she/he can exercise, determines the probability of deviance occurring as well as the likely type of deviance.
Criminologist	A criminologist is often defined as someone who studies the aetiology of crime, criminal behavior, types of crime, and social, cultural and media reactions to crime.
Capitalism	Capitalism is an economic system in which the means of production are owned mostly privately, and capital is invested in the production, distribution and other trade of goods and services, for profit in a competitive free market.
Criminal justice	Criminal justice refers to the system used by government to maintain social control, enforce laws, and administer justice. Law enforcement (police), courts, and corrections are the primary agencies charged with these responsibilities.
Jurisdiction	Jurisdiction refers to every kind of judicial action; the authority of courts and judicial officers to decide cases.
Racism	Racism is a belief in the moral or biological superiority of one race or ethnic group over another or others.
Alienation	In sociology and critical social theory, alienation refers to the individual's estrangement from traditional community and others in general.
Solidarity	Solidarity in sociology refers to the feeling or condition of unity based on common goals,

Go to **Cram101.com** for the Practice Tests for this Chapter.

Go to **Cram101.com** for the Practice Tests for this Chapter.
And, **NEVER** highlight a book again!

	interests, and sympathies among a group's members. Solidarity refers to the ties in a society - social relations - that bind people to one another.
Sanction	A punishment for nonconformity that reinforces socially approved forms of behavior is a sanction.
Norm	In sociology, a norm, or social norm, is a rule that is socially enforced. Social sanctioning is what distinguishes norms from other cultural products such as meaning and values.
Conflict theory	Conflict theory or conflict perspective refers to a theory that conflict is normal and that the task is not to eliminate conflict but to learn to control it so that it becomes constructive.
Criminal law	Criminal law (also known as penal law) is the body of statutory and common law that deals with crime and the legal punishment of criminal offenses. There are four theories of criminal justice: punishment, deterrence, incapacitation, and rehabilitation.
Social control	A social mechanism that regulates individual and group behavior through sanctions and rewards is a social control.
Means of production	Means of production are the materials, tools and other instruments used by workers to make products. This includes: machines, tools materials, plant and equipment, land, raw materials, money, power generation, and so on: anything necessary for labor to produce.
Empirical research	Empirical research is any research that bases its findings on direct or indirect observation as its test of reality. Such research may also be conducted according to hypothetico-deductive procedures, such as those developed from the work of R. A. Fisher.
Ideology	Ideology refers to shared ideas or beliefs which serve to justify and support the interests of a particular group or organizations.

Go to **Cram101.com** for the Practice Tests for this Chapter.
And, **NEVER** highlight a book again!

Printed in the United States
122925LV00001B/183-184/A

9 781428 817111